The Canadian Guide to Managing the Media

Revised Edition

Ed Shiller

Prentice Hall Canada Inc., Scarborough Ontario

To my wife, Rosemary, and my children, David, Jennifer and Lisa, who make it all worthwhile.

Canadian Cataloguing in Publication Data

Shiller, Ed, 1942–
The Canadian guide to managing the media

Revised edition.
ISBN 0-13-324724-4

1. Mass media and business – Canada. 2. Public relations – Canada.
I. Title.

HD59.S55 1994	659.2	C94-931457-9

Prentice-Hall, Inc., Englewood Cliffs, New Jersey
Prentice-Hall International (UK) Limited, London
Prentice-Hall of Australia, Pty. Limited, Sydney
Prentice-Hall Hispanoamericana, S.A., Mexico City
Prentice-Hall of India Private Limited, New Delhi
Prentice-Hall of Japan, Inc., Tokyo
Simon & Schuster Asia Private Limited, Singapore
Editora Prentice-Hall do Brasil, Ltda., Rio de Janeiro

ISBN 0-13-324724-4

Acquisitions Editor: Suzanne Tyson
Production Editor: Kelly Dickson
Copy Editor: Michael Rowan
Production Coordinator: Anna Orodi
Cover and Interior Design: Rene Demers
Page Layout: Jaytype

1 2 3 4 5 FP 99

Printed and bound in Canada

Every reasonable effort has been made to obtain permissions for all articles and data used in this edition. If errors or omissions have occurred, they will be corrected in future editions provided written notification has been received by the publisher.

Contents

Preface

The media are everywhere and they are interested in everything.

Gone are the days when a prominent individual, company or government agency could sidestep the media en route to a haven of anonymity. If there is bad news to tell, you can be sure that at least one enterprising reporter will not give up until the story is revealed. The challenge these days is not to run away from the media, but to know how best to face them.

Indeed, successful businesses and business people, political parties and politicians, public policy associations and advocates – all have discovered that they can benefit from initiating positive stories about themselves. They have learned how to use the media to get their messages across to important publics.

The fact is, very few of us can afford to disregard the media. If your stock is sold to the public, the media can brighten or tarnish your image among shareholders, analysts and potential investors.

If the success of your organization depends on the quality and dedication of the people who work for you, positive media coverage is a magnet that will attract the brightest and best in each profession.

Newspaper, radio and television reports of your products and services will reinforce ties with your customers and attract new business.

Do you want more people to know of your activities, achievements and views?

Do you need to rally community support for your operations?

Do you want to influence government policy affecting your company or industry?

Do you want to be regarded as a leader in your field, whether it be business, politics or social reform?

Does public opinion affect the well-being of your organization?

If so, then getting the right kind of media coverage is essential.

Of course, that's easier said than done. As more and more individuals and organizations realize the benefits of positive media coverage, the competition for coverage becomes increasingly intense. Only well-told stories with good news pegs and plenty of relevant background material will catch the eye of harried editors drowning under a cascade of news releases and other promotional material. And only concise and pithy comments, spoken distinctly and with credibility, will earn a precious few seconds of air time on the evening news.

To "manage" the media is not to dictate to reporters and editors what they should or should not print or say about you. No one can or should try to do that in a free society. Managing the media is, however, knowing what you'd like the media to report about you and knowing how to tell your story in such a way that the media will likely report it the way you want.

Managing the media is, in effect, competing effectively against the myriad other messages that vie for media attention. And that holds true whether you are initiating coverage of your positive achievements or trying to minimize damage from potentially harmful stories.

The Canadian Guide to Managing the Media, and the course I teach on this subject, are products of my ever-increasing experience as a publicist and public relations professional. They grow and evolve in tandem with the knowledge and wisdom I gain every day from my work as a communications consultant and as a teacher of media relations. I rarely complete a project or give a course without gaining new insights into my profession and how to improve my practice of it.

During my years as a public relations executive, I discovered that many otherwise competent practitioners lack some of the skills that effective media relations requires, either because, as former journalists, they have yet to adapt sufficiently to their new environment or, as individuals trained only in public relations, they simply do not yet know the media and the ways of journalism well enough.

My media relations course grew out of these realizations, and *The Canadian Guide to Managing the Media* grew out of the course.

Like the course, this book is directed at a fairly wide audience. Anyone who might, does or should come in contact with the media will benefit, especially from the chapters on how to deal with the media and how to prepare for and give interviews. In today's world, when the media are increasingly aggressive about getting their stories directly from the experts, and when decision makers – controllers, marketers, engineers, lawyers, executives – in both the public and private sectors are called upon to speak publicly on behalf of their organizations – everyone must have at least a passing familiarity with media relations. This book is written for them.

It is also written for the communications professional – the public relations practitioner. Here, too, *The Canadian Guide to Managing the Media* casts a wide net. For the public relations novice, it can serve as a hands-on manual, leading him or her through the often trying and unpredictable turns of media relations. For the seasoned practitioner, it can either fill the gaps that seem to plague us all, no matter how much experience we may have, or provide refreshing insights into our ever-evolving profession.

In this revised edition, I have made a few changes that reflect some of the new experiences I have had in the past years and the effect they have had on my thinking. Most notably, I have devoted an entire chapter to crisis communications, and have updated the section dealing with media directories to reflect the many improvements that have been made to them in the past several years.

The media themselves change, as do the services offered to media relations practitioners. I have tried to keep abreast of the most significant developments and to modify and update *The Canadian Guide to Managing the Media* accordingly.

Ed Shiller
Toronto

Acknowledgements

No book is entirely the work of one person. Authors rely on the help and advice of many well-meaning people, and I am no exception. First, there are the many dozens of public relations practitioners and corporate executives who have taken my course on managing the media. I have learned from their experiences, from their evaluation of the course and from their critiques of evolving drafts of this book.

Many of the reporters and editors with whom I come into daily contact in my capacity as a media relations consultant have shared their observations and gripes about the practice of public relations. I am forever grateful for their viewpoints and for the encouragement they have often given me. As one of them once remarked, "the next time some flack wastes my time with an idiotic news release or unnecessary phone call, I'll tell 'em to take your course."

Rosemary Shiller, my wife, business partner and colleague, has been a patient and wise sounding board throughout. Her comments have added greatly to whatever cogency *The Canadian Guide to Managing the Media* may possess.

I would also like to thank Herb Hilderley for his initial willingness to review the initial manuscript, his subsequent decision to publish this book and his continuing guidance during the inevitably gruelling editorial and production process; Nathan Rudyk for his insightful criticism and constructive suggestions for improving the original manuscript; and Greg Cable, the editor of the first edition, whose keen intelligence and well-developed sense of logic helped shape the final draft.

While I may ascribe many of the good qualities of *The Canadian Guide to Managing the Media* to the wisdom and perseverance of others, I still bear full responsibility for any of its deficiencies. I sincerely hope, however, that the former outweigh the latter.

Why Deal With The Media? 1

Newspapers, magazines, radio and television are the only practical means at your disposal for reaching mass audiences – for broadcasting your message. It makes sense, therefore, for media relations to hold a prominent position in your overall communications plan. In fact, any sales, marketing, recruitment, investor relations, government relations, employee relations or community relations program can be improved by effective use of the media.

Most organizations recognize the media's power and influence. A manufacturer advertises its products. A public interest group places an ad calling for legislation to rally public support for its position. A company develops an ad campaign to promote its corporate image. Governments advertise their programs and achievements to inform the public about available services and to win the goodwill of the electorate.

That's using the media. You buy space in a newspaper or magazine or air time on a radio or TV station, and you use it to get your message across.

Media relations is very much like that.

Except that you don't pay the newspaper or TV network to run your message. You get them to run it free, because it's in their best interest to do so. And it's in their best interest to do so because news is their business, and you're giving them news.

Advertising and Media Relations

Advertising and media relations, then, are really two sides of the same coin, and that coin is getting your message across to key publics, the people who are important to you.

There are differences, though, between an advertisement you place in the paper and a news article you want the paper to write about you.

An ad is a paid message, and as such, has a perceived bias. Whatever its merits – and advertising has lots of merits – objectivity is not one of them. When you place an ad that says your widgets are the best thing since the silicon chip, everyone knows that you're blowing your own horn. But when a reporter writes that your widgets are absolutely terrific, that's someone else blowing your horn. And that gives the message greater credibility.

Think about it. What will bring more potential homebuyers to your model homes – an ad in the Saturday real estate section touting your new subdivision, or a news feature bylined by the real estate writer?

There's another, more important, difference between an ad and a news piece. With an ad, you've got complete control. You write the message, you design the way it's presented, you designate the medium in which the ad will be run and you determine when and how it will be published or broadcast.

You have full and complete control over the dissemination of your message, and if you use that control effectively, you can more than offset any loss of credibility resulting from the implied bias of your ad. The style of your copy and the texture of your design can be honed to elicit the emotional response you want, and that emotional response will lead to the action you want. That's what you pay for with an ad.

And that points up the problem with getting news coverage. You don't have control. You don't control what the reporter writes, what the paper prints or what the TV or radio station broadcasts. You can't dictate that words with positive overtones be used and that emotionally charged words be discarded. You don't generate the layout and design, so you can't be sure that the subtle influence of graphics will work for you or against you.

That's where media relations comes in.

Can You Gain Control?

Other than buying space or time, nothing can guarantee complete control over the media. But the better your media relations programs and skills, the greater the control you will have.

The goal of media relations, therefore, is to maximize your control over the media.

It is to manage the media by improving the odds that your message will be reported accurately, completely and credibly.

Truth or Consequences

I worked as a reporter and editor for newspapers, magazines and radio for 15 years before going into public relations. And the many years I've spent on each side of the communications fence have confirmed that most media people are honest, dedicated and sincere professionals driven by a compelling desire to unearth and report the truth. At the same time, all are human and fallible. Unlike most of us, a reporter cannot easily hide a mistake. It's printed or broadcast for all to see, and for some to lament. Then too, there are the few bad apples – the reporter or editor who will subordinate the truth to sensationalism, who will display cruel wit at the expense of fairness or be blinded by prejudice.

Unfortunately, many of us have had bad experiences in dealing with the media. We've been misquoted or quoted out of context, we've been hounded for stories we would rather keep quiet and we've seen reporters or editors distort or sensationalize seemingly straightforward events. It doesn't matter that the instances of fair and honest reporting vastly outnumber the times we've been burned, for one bad encounter can engender hardened cynicism about the media.

The relationship between executive, on the one hand, and journalist, on the other, can become fractured by mutual antagonism, suspicion and distrust. The consequences of this can be devastating. When the media and their primary sources of information become estranged, only the truth will suffer. The informed source – the source upon which good journalism is founded – remains silent, forcing the journalist to explore less desirable avenues such as ill-informed outsiders, disgruntled employees, headline seekers, and a host of others whose lack of accurate or comprehensive information is sadly augmented by a compulsion to offend and besmirch.

By refusing to work effectively with the media, you – the executive, the technical expert or communications professional – will merely promote inaccurate and misleading journalism, and that will eventually erode the underpinnings of our democracy. A misinformed public is ill-equipped to participate constructively or intelligently in the political decision-making process. How do you pick the best candidates for political office when you don't have a decent understanding of the issues upon which the parties are campaigning?

Inaccurate and misleading journalism also erodes the underpinnings of our economy. The business decisions that all of us make every day, in our various roles as employees, investors or entrepreneurs, are based in large measure on the information we glean from radio, television, daily newspapers and specialized magazines.

If we don't have truthful and complete information, the quality of our decisions will suffer.

The price of substandard media coverage, therefore, is paid not necessarily by the media themselves, but by those who rely upon the media for the information needed to function effectively in a highly complex and ever-changing political and economic climate.

Looked at from this perspective, managing the media is not an option. It's an imperative.

Media Relations and Corporate Strategy

Because the media are such an important vehicle for getting your message across to the people upon whom your well-being depends, a good media relations strategy must form part of your overall corporate strategy. It must become an integral part of your organizational planning process.

What are you as a company?

Are you the Cadillac of your industry, serving the carriage trade? Or are you the K-cars – fine and reliable products designed without frills for less affluent consumers? Or do you want to switch from one camp to the other?

Are you a well-run organization with a bright future? Are you an industry leader, developing new technologies and new products? Or are you an industry follower, using what others develop and discover?

Do people regard your hiring practices, working conditions and compensation packages as fair and competitive? Are you viewed as a caring company, concerned about the well-being of your community and the protection of our shared environment?

Whatever your niche or whatever you'd like it to be, you've got to communicate that. And not just to your customers, but to myriad other publics. You not only need people to buy your widgets, you also need people to design them, manufacture them, package them, sell them and transport them to market. You need people to invest in your company. And you'd better make sure that the government doesn't tax you out of existence, or that tariff and nontariff barriers don't deny you access to lucrative markets within Canada or around the world.

If you're a trade or industry association, you also manufacture a product. It may not be a microchip, a mortgage or a car door handle, but it's a product nonetheless. You're manufacturing information that's needed by your members, and you're manufacturing persuasion as you lobby government to act in the best interests of your members. If you're a government agency, your products are the many and varied services you provide to the public.

Whatever the nature of your activities, you've got to communicate:
- to project your image and to ensure that people perceive you the way you want to be perceived;
- to earn the confidence of investors, clients or voters;
- to attract the skilled employees you need;
- to win the acceptance and support of your community;
- to influence the formulation and implementation of public policy that can affect your business or your members.

Managing the media is as important to you as managing the manufacture of your products, the quality of your service and the effectiveness of your marketing and sales team.

Practicing Effective Media Relations   2

Media relations involves a host of activities. Practicing successful media relations requires an assortment of tools and a variety of mind sets.

In addition to written and oral skills, effective media relations requires a detailed knowledge of who the media are and how they work, as well as a highly developed ability to think and exercise judgement.

You've got to know how to write – how to take a sentence that may be ungrammatical or clumsily written and put it into correct and flowing English. You must know the proper form in which media material should be presented – how to format a news release with the proper style for release date, headline, dateline, page footers and contact names. And you have to know how to get your material into the hands of the media. The list goes on, and constitutes an impressive job description.

As indispensable as these skills are, however, they are primarily mechanical and routine. They make up only one side of media relations. You learn them, in much the same way a stenographer learns shorthand and the workings of a word processor or the way in which a payroll clerk learns how to process a pile of data so that your take-home pay, unemployment insurance premium and tax and pension contribution are all properly recorded and end up in the right pockets.

Good media relations requires something more. To do a good job, you've also got to develop and use demanding intellectual skills. You have to be an adept corporate strategist and you've got to play the roles of both reporter and editor.

This means learning how to detect a good news story and how to make a potentially good story newsworthy. The opening of a new production facility is news, but what makes it newsworthy? Is it the contribution it will make to your company's overall earnings? Is it the number of new jobs it will create? Is it the contribution it will make to solving a gnawing environmental problem? Is it the use of new technology?

To arrive at the right answer, you must be thoroughly versed in the operations and performance of your organization, its relationships with its various publics, and its short- and long-term goals.

Since very few of us have this knowledge at our fingertips, you have to know what questions to ask and of whom.

And then comes the hard part – taking all the information you've gathered, selecting what can be used to advance your organization's objectives, then digesting it, moulding it and trimming it into the well-honed tool of a comprehensive media relations program.

The Essential Elements

To perform these operations well, you require keen imagination and judgement, both to know what should be told through the media and to evaluate the impact of media coverage on your organization. You need a keen curiosity and tenacity to get the information you need, and keen skills and intelligence to distil the essential meaning of that information and transform it into an effective media tool.

This is thinking, and it is the most important part of good media relations. Unfortunately, of all the attributes of a good media relations manager or practitioner, the ability to think is the one most often ignored by the people who need good media relations the most.

How often have you been handed a draft news release with the explicit instruction, "Just check it for spelling and punctuation, but don't tamper with it. Our lawyers and accountants have gone over it very carefully and it's very important that the media report it exactly as it's written"?

Well, the media won't report it "exactly as it's written" – if, indeed, they report it at all – unless your news release and supporting materials adhere to accepted journalistic standards and principles. What might impress a judge in a court of law may simply confuse and alienate an editor or reporter.

Your job as a media relations expert is to know the quality and quantity of media coverage you will most likely get from the various newsworthy events generated by your organization; it is to exercise good news judgement and to apply good reportorial skills in order to identify good media opportunities and to maximize the possibilities for favourable media coverage.

Your company, trade association or government agency should realize that effective media relations requires the application of skills and intelligence that are equal in degree to those of any other department, whether it be human resources, accounting, law or engineering. And as a media relations person, you should have the same degree of professional recognition and latitude afforded these other disciplines.

Like so many human endeavours, media relations is part science and part art, part rules and regulations and part innovation and initiative.

The Basic Questions

A good way to start acquiring the knowledge and developing the skills for an effective media relations program is to ask the fundamental questions of good journalism, the five Ws:

- Why pursue an active media relations program?
- Who are the media and how should you treat them?
- When should you tell your story to the media and when should you not?
- What makes something newsworthy?
- What are the components of a media relations program?
- Where do you want your story told?

There are also some very important "Hows." How do you reach the right media to tell your story? How do you write a news release? How do you prepare for and give interviews?

By understanding the answers to these questions, the media relations professional will gain the knowledge and skills needed to do the job properly. But, to be useful, information also has to be relevant. It must fit into a discernible context and be part of a process. Acquiring knowledge is only the first step. You then have to learn how to apply that knowledge effectively.

The Critical Path

To design and implement a good media relations program you should follow a 10-step critical path.

The first step is to identify the major goals and objectives of your organization. I'm not talking here about your communications objectives – they will come later, when you evaluate specific media relations opportunities – but the overall goals and objectives of the organization for which you work. Your company may want to increase its market share from 10 per cent to 15 per cent. It may plan to integrate vertically by expanding from production of raw materials into the manufacture of the finished product. It may plan to raise $100 million in an equity issue. Or it may need to increase productivity, downsize its workforce or renegotiate its bank debt.

To have any value whatsoever, your media relations program must contribute to the attainment of these broad organizational objectives. Setting a communications goal, for example, of getting five positive stories about your CEO in the Report on Business during the next year may or may not be a good thing. Certainly, in an abstract sense, having somebody say something nice about you is better than having them say nothing at all. But are those five glowing stories the most effective communications vehicle for increasing your company's market share or bringing you closer to your goal of vertical integration? Unless you are thoroughly familiar with those goals, you will only be able to give a vague answer to that question, saying, "positive exposure, any positive exposure, must surely be a help." Indeed, it would. But would it be the most help for the time, effort and money expended? Probably not.

Once you've identified your organization's overall goals and objectives, you can move on to the second step – identifying and analyzing the publics whose support or acquiescence are important to the attainment of those goals and objectives.

To carry on with one example, to expand your market share, your communications program will obviously have to reach at least three distinct groups in the marketplace: Those people who have never bought the goods and services you're selling, those who are buying from your competitors, and your existing customers (you want them to stay with you and to buy more).

But don't stop there. To increase its market penetration, your company may also have determined that it must improve its competitiveness by increasing the productivity of the workforce. Your employees now become an essential public, since you'll have to persuade them to produce more goods for each dollar they are paid. You'll have to motivate them to work harder and make fewer mistakes. Highly efficient management is often a vital ingredient in worker productivity, so you might also now add line managers to your list of publics.

Let's assume, as well, that your company wants to improve product quality as a means of moving closer to its goal of increasing market share. It may do this by buying technology, engaging in joint-venture research projects or expanding in-house research capabilities. You would have one set of publics if you wanted to attract joint-venture partners, another if you were trying to hire experienced scientists to work at the company's research laboratory.

Knowing who your publics are is only part of the battle. You must also analyze these publics to gain a clear understanding of how they are acting now, what perceptions or attitudes are making them act that way, how you would like them to act and what new perceptions or attitudes will make them act the way you want them to.

Let's say that your organization needs to borrow $20 million from its bank. If the bank is willing to lend the money, there really is nothing specific that you must do on the communications front to attain that objective. Your key public is already doing what you want it to do. But let's suppose that the organization is meeting resistance from the bank. In this case, before you can communicate (through the media or otherwise) you must determine why the bank doesn't want to lend the money. What's in the minds of the key bankers? It's pretty likely that they doubt your organization will be able to repay the loan. Let's postulate that they're also concerned that making the loan might create other problems for the bank, say, because your organization or others similar to yours have been identified with the unpopular side of a major controversy, and the bank simply doesn't want to look bad.

Given these circumstances, your communications task is two-fold: first, to persuade the bank that your organization has sufficient financial resources to repay the loan; second, to get the bank to believe that it will earn widespread praise for supporting your organization – not only because you are financially sound, but also because you are involved in worthy activities. (See "Reaching Out to Your Publics" in Chapter 3 for a few more thoughts on the subject of publics.)

So now you thoroughly understand where the organization wants to go (its goals and objectives) and the various publics that will help bring it there. The third step in the critical path is to identify those issues and activities about which publicity could help induce those publics to think and act the way you want them to.

To help create the specific attitudes that will get the bank to lend the $20 million, consult your financial people to identify developments that will demonstrate your organization's financial strength and future prospects. At the same time, analyze your organization's overall activities to identify the specific ways in which they benefit the public.

Or, in the case of the company that wants to increase market share, you may want me, the customer, to stop buying your competitor's product and start buying yours. Working closely with your company's sales and marketing department, you may determine that price is a significant factor in consumer behaviour. You've now identified an issue that you could publicize. Alternatively, your potential customers may be more concerned about quality than price; so that would be the issue to concentrate on.

To attract top-notch scientists you may want to publicize your company's compensation package and working conditions, but you may also want to demonstrate how working for your company may enhance professional standing and social status. So you might decide to build a communications program around the awards and honours received by your employees or the many innovations your company has made over the years and is continuing to make today.

Having fixed on a few issues and activities, you will now take the fourth step along the critical path by identifying the specific key points about each issue that will most effectively influence the publics you've identified. There is one simple rule here: Highlight the benefits that will accrue to the publics you want to reach. You're not only going to tell me that your company is an innovator in its field. You are going to explain how this would offer me exciting career opportunities in an environment that encourages individual creativity and achievement.

Since you want the media to carry your message to your key publics, that message must be one that the media do, indeed, want to print or broadcast. In essence, the topic and the specific key points you wish to publicize must not only be chosen because of the positive effects they will have on your publics, they must also be newsworthy.

To put it another way, consider the media as one of your key publics. To help you attain one or more of your organizational objectives, you want this public – the media – to publish certain messages. To get the media to do that, the media must perceive a benefit to themselves. Since the media thrive on news, the benefit accrues from the newsworthiness of the messages you want printed or broadcast. (For further discussion, see "What Makes a Story Newsworthy?" in Chapter 9.)

Step five is to identify the media that will best carry these messages to your chosen publics. If you want to recruit recent graduates, then the network of college and university newspapers and radio stations comprises your essential media. If you want to reach people already well established in their fields, then concentrate on the trade and business press. If you want to gain local support for a controversial business venture in, say, northern Ontario, then the community newspapers in the area would be important. But do not lose sight of the effect that positive coverage in the mass media (radio, television and daily newspapers) can have on virtually any public. Most initiatives involve a wide variety of media. (See Chapter 6 for information about media directories and compiling your own media lists.)

Next, your sixth step, you've got to prepare or gather the materials that should go to the media you've selected. This is your media information kit, which should contain information that meets two essential criteria: It must establish the key points you want to make, and it must be usable by the media. To meet the latter criterion, your kit must be brief so that it can be clearly understood and evaluated by busy and often harried journalists, and it must be written in a way that meets good journalistic standards. (For further discussion of media information kits, see Chapter 9.)

The seventh step is to distribute these materials to the media by the most appropriate means. You'll have to decide how quickly your story should be delivered, whether the various media should receive it simultaneously, which parts of your kit should go to which media and how you should follow up. (For further discussion, see "Media Distribution Methods" in Chapter 6.)

In some cases, you may decide that the most effective coverage will result if the media interview a prominent person within your organization. If so, you've arrived at step number eight. This type of program involves a great deal of personal contact with reporters and editors, and is often one that generates the most friction and ill will. Too often, PR people become high-pressure salespeople trying to push reporters into covering events in which neither they and their editors, nor their readers, viewers or listeners have any interest. Your job, as an effective media relations practitioner, is to use your own good news judgement along with hefty doses of tact and diplomacy to bring good stories to the attention of the media and then to let them pick up the ball or let it lie. (For the specific steps to follow, see "Arranging Media Interviews" in Chapter 8.)

In any event, you should always be prepared for the interview that the reporter wants to initiate, which brings you to the ninth step. Just because you know a subject well doesn't mean that you can give a good interview on it. Just because you spent 30 years developing the technology that will reduce sulphur dioxide emissions from your company's smokestack doesn't mean that you will be able to explain that technology in 15 seconds while also conveying the idea that your company is a good corporate citizen committed to protecting the environment. That is a skill that takes study and practice to learn well. (Chapter 8 delves more deeply into the subject of giving media interviews.)

Finally, for the tenth step, you will want to evaluate the media coverage you received, and here is where your communications (as opposed to organizational) goals and objectives come into play. Not every story is a page-one blockbuster. Most are mundane and minor or have an appeal to a particular segment of society. If you followed steps three and four, you will have already evaluated the newsworthiness of your story and will have pursued it only if you're confident that it will reach and have a positive effect on one or more of your selected publics. Knowing this, you will develop realistic expectations of the coverage your story will get. By monitoring that coverage, both in terms of its scope and nature, you will be able to determine with a reasonable degree of accuracy how effective your efforts really were.

Completing these steps for any given situation can take as little as a day or two or as long as several weeks or months. It all depends on the nature of the subject matter you're dealing with, your familiarity with it, the type of coverage you want and believe you can achieve and, most importantly, your general state of readiness. (See Chapter 13 for specific ways in which you can monitor and evaluate your media coverage.)

Knowing Your Organization

Aside from possessing the basic skills – knowing the who, what, when, where, why and how of media relations – readiness also requires extensive knowledge of what your organization does, where it wants to go and the obstacles it must overcome to reach its short- and long-term goals. You should be constantly picking the brains of the key people in your organization.

If you work in an enlightened environment, the senior public relations or public affairs people already meet regularly with top management, which keeps them informed and seeks their views on how new developments can be used to help achieve organizational objectives.

This is a policy function and, unfortunately, many organizations don't believe that their PR people should get involved in broad policy planning. If you are in that situation, your job is more difficult, but not hopeless. If top management won't inform you or seek your advice, you'll just have to use less formal lines of communication to get the information you need to plan an effective media relations program or activity. And you will have to show initiative and perhaps a little aggressiveness in bringing your media relations proposals to management attention.

Get to know the key managers in other departments. Learn about the company's financial situation over lunch with the controller. A chat with the chief engineer may tip you off to a new manufacturing process. From the marketing people you'll get to know what conditions have the greatest impact on sales. By talking to staff lawyers and personnel people, you'll gain invaluable insights into how employees, community groups and other important publics view your organization.

Such information may seem to have little to do directly with acquiring good media relations skills. But without it, you'll be severely handicapped. Knowledge is the key that unlocks the gate to the critical path.

Gathering information is part of an inductive process – each bit of data helps you piece together such generalities as your organization's major goals and objectives, the kinds of issues and developments that you should be publicizing to help achieve them, and the various publics whose perceptions or attitudes you will have to change.

Applying your knowledge is a deductive process. The way you should handle the publicity for a particular development or event will follow, in large measure, from the inductive conclusions you've reached.

In essence, the information you've gathered sensitizes you to the needs and concerns of the various departments in your organization. As a result, you will be better equipped to ensure that any news you generate will help meet those needs and concerns.

You can generate news passively or actively. You can wait for management to come to you with an item to publicize, or you can come up with your own ideas and sell them to management. In either case, the more you know of your organization's operations and aspirations, the more effective and efficient your media relations activities will be.

As Mr. Spock would say, it's all very logical.

Gaining Credibility Inside

What you'll often find – if you haven't already suffered the indignity – is that senior management will often ignore your advice, reject your ideas or simply refuse to entertain them in the first place.

One indication of the low professional esteem in which many organizations hold the public relations function is their self-destructive habit of appointing people with absolutely no public relations experience to sensitive public relations positions. Think about it. If you're not only new to the job but new to the profession, you have no more experience in PR than any senior manager with whom you may come in contact. Given this situation, how much respect and credibility can you command?

If you do nothing to change this initial situation, the perception of you as inexperienced, and thus ineffective, will persist and solidify. You will forever be relegated to the lowly position of PR gofer. If you ever manage to persuade senior management of your skill and competence, it will, in their eyes, be the skill and competence of the recruit – the lowly private – not the officer. You may come to be seen as reliable, perhaps, even as an asset to the organization. But your role will remain passive, your advice, if asked for, will be ignored, and sooner or later you will eventually become frustrated, angry and alienated.

You're not alone. We've all been through it. And we all know what you're feeling. Unfortunately, there is no easy way out. No panacea. You can build credibility with your senior management team and you can build acceptance for your programs and approvals for their budgets. But it will take time.

The first step on this arduous journey is to understand where your management nemesis is coming from. To the men and women who run the accounting, legal, human resources, marketing and production departments, public relations does not enjoy professional status. Anyone can do it, they believe, because it merely involves being nice to people, polishing the words and the thoughts that others give you and generally behaving in such a way that no one outside the organization will ever get a glimpse of what really goes on inside. And, as we all know, those skills can be summed up in a single phrase: the art of bullshit. As the chief financial officer of a large Toronto-based company remarked in response to a word of praise about how sharp the company's public relations counsel was: "Sharp, hell. We all know what it takes to be a PR man."

The second step is to dispel this myth of the modern public relations practitioner as sleazy hack. You're in a profession that requires an impressive array of skills and a unique combination of intelligence and intuition.

So, if you don't already possess the prerequisites of your profession, acquire them. Make a show of acquiring them. Do little things, like installing bookshelves in your office and then filling them with books, magazines and brochures on PR topics (and, of course, you might even read them).

Take public relations courses and attend symposiums. Universities, community colleges, professional associations and individual consulting firms offer an ever-widening range of courses dealing with such topics as media relations, interview skills, business writing, graphics, annual reports, crisis communications, audio-visual techniques and opportunities, presentation skills — you name it, there's probably a course for it.

Join the Canadian Public Relations Society, the International Association of Business Communicators or both, then display your framed certificate of membership proudly on your office wall, and the latest issue of their periodical on your bookshelf.

So there you are. You've acquired the knowledge and skills essential to your profession. You can now implement creative public relations programs that will enhance the standing of your organization among its most important publics, thereby helping it achieve its most sought-after goals.

Or can you? You know what you can do, and I know what you can do. But does your President or Chief Financial Officer? Probably not. So tell them.

The best way of doing that is to show them. Debating isn't always the most effective approach, but a calm, reasoned firmness often is. If, for example, you believe the best way to tell your story is through a news release, don't wait for formal approval from the top before penning one. You may lose that argument and never get the project launched. Instead, go with your convictions and draft the release the way it should be written. Clearly enunciate your reasons for doing so, then present the finished product along with your cogent arguments to the boss. Start your discussion with the actual product in hand, not before it's produced.

If you believe an executive's speech would make a good news story, don't waste time trying to explain what you would like to do to get coverage – just do it. Distribute the speech to the appropriate media and do your best to arrange the most favourable and widespread coverage possible. Then show off the results. (Of course, you'd better be pretty certain beforehand that the executive would welcome media coverage of his or her remarks.)

Identify a key person on the management team. Choose someone with a lot of clout for whom publicity would be both welcome and beneficial, say, that Chief Financial Officer with the disparaging view of public relations and its practitioners. Then build a mini-PR program around him. Arrange for a respected journal to write a profile of this up-and-coming young executive based on his innovative approach to bean-counting or whatever. He'll likely relish the publicity and, since you delivered the goods, he'll grant you a measure of respect and consideration you didn't enjoy before. You may not change his inner attitudes about PR people, but he will recognize where his self-interest lies.

You may find that the attitudes many executives hold about PR people are based more on bad experiences with the media than with any ingrained prejudice against public relations. For these people, decent media coverage will eventually soften their aversion to the media and, in the process, to the effective use of public relations in general.

The key word here, however, is "eventually." Changing attitudes and building credibility is not an overnight thing. It takes time and perseverance. If you can slog it out for a year or so, you've probably got it made. If you're getting nowhere after your second summer, start planning a major move.

Hiring Outside Consultants

Outside consultants have it easy by comparison. They enter the organization with an abundance of what industrial psychologists like to call "face credibility." Consultants, by definition, know more than you, otherwise you wouldn't hire them in the first place. They'd never get past the receptionist. There's a simple, but vital, human foible at work here. We tend to give greater value to the advice we pay for than the advice we get free (that's why it rarely pays for a consultant to offer discounts).

Two critical questions are when to hire outside consultants and how to use them effectively. All too often, consultants are hired unnecessarily and utilized inefficiently or counterproductively. So here are a few tips.

- Don't go for overkill. Hire only what you need and no more. If you want a writer for your annual report, then hire a freelance writer. Don't approach a large PR firm. You'll just end up paying thousands of dollars extra for a bunch of middlemen whose only contribution to the project will be to block effective communication with the writer.
- Know your own capabilities. Don't assume automatically that because a person is a consultant, he or she knows more about PR than you do. If you're a trained professional, you can probably handle anything just as well as any outside consultant, assuming you have the time.
- Don't be bamboozled by glitz and hype. Most public relations consultants are honest, competent people who are sincerely dedicated to serving the best interests of their clients. But individual consultants and public relations firms sometimes get their priorities mixed up and will try to sell the client on a program that would serve more to showcase their own virtuosity than meet the communications goals of the client.

Years ago, when I was working for a large trade association, we went to an outside communications firm for help in promoting an executive symposium. They came back with an elaborate concept based on the theme "Vision 2000." They provided us with what looked like a custom-designed program, complete with graphic and video concepts that seemed to fit well with the topic of the symposium. But when we went to their studio to examine the proposal in more detail, we discovered that the "customized" video was a canned product that they wanted to rent at a fee of $8,000 for a single showing ($12,000 if they added the name of our organization).

The "Vision 2000" theme? That was the name already on the video. And the supposedly custom-designed graphics? Well, they, too, were taken off the shelf, repeating the graphic theme of "Vision 2000." We weren't offered advice on how to ensure that the symposium would be a success from the organization's point of view. Instead, we were being sold a bill of goods designed to showcase the communications company.

- Provide your outside counsel with clear direction. Ideally, an outside public relations consultant or PR firm should report to the in-house PR professional, for the simple reason that it takes one professional to evaluate the concepts, budgets, time frames and work of another. Indeed, most bamboozling takes place between an outside professional and an inside amateur. Furthermore, the outside professional will be less familiar with the goals, history and culture of the organization – a lack of knowledge that will hamper the formulation and implementation of any communications program. It is essential that an in-house PR person fill in these gaps in knowledge and experience.

- Make sure you know who is actually going to be doing the work for you. The representative of the PR firm making the presentation to you may be articulate, knowledgeable, intelligent and everything else wonderful. But is he or she the person who is actually going to be servicing your account once the contract is signed? Find out, and don't settle for second best. If you like the sample brochure, speech, news release or annual report shown by the firm's rep, then insist that the same people who produced those products produce yours. Of course, if all you want is a good writer or designer, why go to a large PR firm in the first place? Just go out and engage a good freelancer. It'll be much cheaper and less time-consuming.

- Avoid the "Aunt Tilley" syndrome. "Hey," suggests the chief bottle washer, "why spend a bundle on some outside consultant, when my cousin George loves to write. I'm sure he'd be great to do this year's annual report." Fine, if you want to settle for first place in this year's "best-effort-by-an-amateur" contest. Good professionals are just that: good professionals. Amateurs are just that: amateurs.

IN BRIEF

Planning a Media Relations Program

The Critical Path

1. Identify your major organizational goals and objectives.
2. Identify and analyze the key publics you want to reach.
3. Identify the activities or issues on which publicity would help advance your organization's goals and objectives.
4. Identify the key points you want to publicize.
5. Identify the media that will best carry your message.
6. Prepare or gather the materials for the media.
7. Distribute those materials by the most appropriate means.
8. Arrange for media interviews, if appropriate.
9. Prepare for media interviews.
10. Evaluate the media coverage you received.

Why Be Proactive?   3

When should you initiate media coverage? When should you not?

Your answers to these questions will determine the nature and effectiveness of your media relations activities. Be passive, and you will likely end up reacting to events and struggling to put out potentially damaging fires. Take the initiative, and you'll set the tone of coverage of your organization and end up preventing fires. These two extremes exemplify the difference between a reactive program and a proactive program.

In most cases, I advocate being proactive.

Why? Because we live in a highly competitive world.

As a private-sector company, you will want the public to buy your products, not your competitors'. You want to attract the best employees. And of course, you want to operate in an economic and political climate that will encourage investment.

As a trade association, you will want to be more credible and more influential than groups representing opposing interests.

As a university, you will be vying with other educational institutions to attract the best students, teachers, endowments and government grants.

As government, you will not only compete for votes at election time, but compete against every public interest group and lobby in ongoing debates on major public policy issues.

Reaching Out to Your Publics

There are people upon whom your livelihood depends, and your story will give them a more positive impression of your organization. This will help boost sales, increase the value of your stock, aid personnel recruitment, raise employee morale, improve relations with communities in which you operate or influence the formulation of public policy that could affect your well-being.

The list of important publics is enormous. For corporations, it can include:

1. Employees.
2. Potential employees.
3. Investment analysts and stockbrokers.
4. Shareholders.
5. Customers.
6. Suppliers.
7. Trade associations.
8. Competitors.
9. Government.
10. Special-interest groups (environmentalists, women's groups, church groups, etc.).
11. The media.

A trade association would share many of the same publics, but would also add members and potential members. Governments would, of course, include voters on the list.

You reach out to these publics by being proactive. You don't wait for the media to sniff out a story and come to you with it. Rather, you initiate positive media coverage yourself by identifying newsworthy aspects of your organization and its operations that lend themselves to positive coverage, then by presenting your ideas to the media in accurate, timely and well-written Media Information Kits.

To help achieve your organization's goals, you try to get the media to convey your message to the audiences that are important to you. And you interest the media in your message by presenting it in a captivating way that will successfully compete with the millions of other messages that vie every day for the attention of your audience.

Fulfilling Disclosure Requirements

There can be many other reasons for being proactive, an important one being that, in many cases, the law demands it. Public companies must report certain financial and other material information as soon as it becomes available to the company. In fact, any corporate developments that may affect the value of a company's stock must be reported to shareholders without undue delay.

Distributing that information to the media is the best way of getting it before investors and potential investors, and sometimes it's the only way to meet statutory requirements. Failure to meet disclosure requirements can result in prosecution and conviction, even if the error was unintentional.

Getting the Story Right

Finally, if you don't tell your story right, someone else may tell it wrong. After all, you don't have exclusive rights to your own story. Just ask Frank Sinatra or Elizabeth Taylor.

Most reporters – and their editors – approach a story with some kind of bias. That's only natural. An editor wouldn't assign a story and a reporter wouldn't be on the phone to you with a barrel full of questions if they hadn't already done some research, formed some opinions about the angle they want to take with the story and developed some expectations about the information they hope to uncover.

The trouble is that in some cases the research may have given the reporter or editor incorrect information that has led to the formulation of unfounded opinions and expectations. The reporter may be filled with misconceptions about you and your organization before ever picking up the phone. Unfortunately, by the time the reporter gets hold of you, those misconceptions may have already settled into firm opinions that you will not be able to shake, even if your facts are correct and well presented. This won't always happen, but it will happen often enough to make you wary of speaking to the media.

I had such an experience. A reporter for the *Winnipeg Free Press*, Ilana Simon, showed up during the lunch break at a recent session of "Managing the Media." The first question she shot at three participants who happened to be there at the time was: "Don't you think $625 is a pretty exorbitant fee to pay for this course?" It went downhill from there.

The answers the reporter got were pretty good. One participant said, "No, the fee is reasonable and it's generally what you have to pay for courses of this type." They all said they liked the course and felt they were getting their money's worth.

The reporter then sat in on the course for a few minutes as the group discussed the importance of responding quickly to reporters' questions with accurate information.

Ms. Simon called the meeting room the next day just as we were breaking up. She seemed to have it in her mind that I was teaching people, especially government people, how to evade the media and cover up stories. The published agenda, it seemed, was a confirmation of the sinister intent of the course.

"You have a section on when not to tell your story to the media. Why do you teach people to cover up stories?" she asked.

I answered that I advise both public- and private-sector organizations to be proactive in their relations with the media. Far from preaching avoidance of the media, I told her I advocate being open and accommodating, and I caution people against telling their stories to the media only when they are driven by an urge to see their name in print or to sensationalize the facts.

No matter. The stories (there were two, on successive days) published in the *Free Press* bore little similarity to the realities I had discussed. As the saying goes, why let the facts stand in the way of a good story?

That's enough to turn you off the media for good. After all, why talk to the media when they are going to distort, misrepresent and misquote? Better never to initiate a media program and to ignore the media whenever they dare call you, right?

Wrong! On several counts. First, giving Ms. Simon the boot would not have prevented the story from being written. I have no doubt that the coverage would have been even less accurate and more biased had I refused to talk to her about the course – and you can be sure that that tidbit would have been mentioned prominently in the story. A cabinet minister hung up on Ms. Simon when she called to ask him about authorizing government employees to take courses like "Managing the Media." How do I know the minister slammed down the phone? Because I read it in the *Free Press*.

Second, cooperating with the reporter gives you avenues of response to erroneous stories that you would not have if you refused to cooperate. I know what I told her, and when my comments were not accurately or fairly reported, I could take my grievance to her and her editor and rightfully demand redress. By having cooperated, I was in a position to argue the merits or demerits of her story with the newspaper's City Editor. Had I refused to grant her the interview, we could not have discussed what was wrong with the story and how it must be corrected. Instead, I would have been told that any inaccuracies in the story were the result of my lack of cooperation and not the fault of the newspaper. The *Free Press* would say it reported the facts it was given, and if I didn't like it, I could lump it.

By granting the interview I had greater influence, not only on the story itself (although that influence may be very slim if the reporter is biased against you from the beginning), but also over any grievance procedure that I might initiate following publication of an inaccurate story.

In the actual case, I discussed my concerns with the City Editor, who agreed to publish a news story the following week based on a new interview with me. We agreed that I should call the paper the following Monday at noon and give the interview, for which I dutifully prepared. I tried to anticipate all the questions I might be asked and I wrote down the answers word-for-word that I wanted to give.

I called the City Editor at the agreed-upon time and, true to his word, he assigned another reporter to conduct the interview. It went well, and according to plan. There were no surprise questions and I felt that I had, at last, set the record straight.

Maybe so. But the story, if it was ever written, never appeared in print.

When that became clear, I had several options: call the City Editor, lodge a complaint with the Press Council, instigate legal proceedings, launch a media campaign of my own to get my story told via the other media in Winnipeg, or do nothing.

In the end, I did nothing. Was that the proper option? Frankly, I don't think so. I was had, and I took it lying down like so many of us who have felt victimized by a less-than-responsible press. The feeling of being used and abused lingered for weeks. Yet I did nothing. Why? Because I believed that the time, effort and money it would have taken to fight the paper was too great. I had to devote my energies to my business, to earning a living. It was a judgement call. I might have decided to pursue the matter and perhaps the *Free Press* would have written that second story after all. Then again, perhaps not.

As an interesting footnote, about six weeks after the interview with the *Free Press*, yet another reporter telephoned me at my Toronto office asking about the course as part of an article she was preparing about government spending on professional development for civil servants. I told her about my experience with the *Free Press*, but agreed to cooperate. She asked about my course and my approach to media relations, questions that I welcomed answering in hopes of finally setting the record straight. To reduce any possibility of being misquoted, I reiterated my answers in an express letter (it was before fax) to the reporter. But alas, not one word of what I said or wrote was reported.

But for those of you who may regard this experience as a lot of sound and fury signifying nothing, think again, for it leads to another point about the advantages of being proactive: By taking the initiative to develop positive stories about your organization, you preempt those editors and reporters who are biased against you out of either malice or ignorance.

With an effective, ongoing media relations program, you will be able to drown out negative stories with positive ones. The positive media coverage you generate will, over time, engender a foundation of goodwill towards your organization, and that goodwill will act as a buffer against any negative coverage you receive. If people have a good feeling about you – if they believe you contribute to the betterment of society, are a good corporate citizen, play an active role in community affairs, treat your employees well and place principles of fairness and honesty above the raw tenets of striving for ever greater profit or power – then they will be more likely to believe the good that is said about you and disbelieve the bad.

The media and the people that work for the media are far from perfect. But you will only be doing yourself and the organization you represent a disservice by using the imperfections of the media as an excuse for shutting them out.

IN BRIEF

Why Be Proactive?

- To project a positive impression of your organization.
- To fulfill your organizational mandate.
- To meet timely disclosure requirements.
- To ensure that your story is told correctly.

Crisis Communications 4

For the sake of argument, let's say that your organization is not obligated by public disclosure requirements and, generally, doesn't have enough to say to the media to justify a proactive media relations program. Does that mean you can disregard the media altogether?

The answer, obviously, is no. A fire in your plant kills three workers and destroys $1 million worth of inventory. Your chairman is called upon to testify in a conflict-of-interest hearing. You've discovered a safety defect and must recall the 10,000 widgets sold within the past six months.

How are you going to handle the flood of media calls? Whether you like it or not, you've got to deal with that crisis. So even if you choose to take a reactive stance in your media relations, you must be prepared for crises; you must develop the capability for crisis communications.

The Crisis Communications Plan

The first thing is to get a crisis communications plan in place before you get a crisis. Here's what will likely happen if you don't have a plan:
- an incident occurs
- no one tells you about it . . .
- but the media find out
- reporters' calls go unanswered because management believes that keeping quiet will stop media coverage
- the resulting media stories are misleading and harmful to your organization
- management finally decides it's time to issue a countering statement
- this is reported . . .

- but so are the counterclaims of those pointing the finger at you.

The crisis has now become a disaster.

Well, the purpose of a crisis communications plan is not to prevent crises – they're going to happen anyway. It is to prevent crises from becoming disasters.

It achieves this aim in two stages. The first is to ensure that you, the communications specialist, are alerted to any situation within your organization that could escalate into a disaster. The second is to provide you with the necessary information, access to senior management and financial and human resources to take the proper corrective action.

The biggest impediment to effective crisis communications is the reluctance of employees to inform their superiors of potentially damaging situations. As undesirable as this may be, it is understandable. Often the person who first knows that something has gone awry – a contaminant got into the bottled water, the gas tanks on late-model pickup trucks were not properly installed, or the odometers on demo cars were turned back – was the person responsible. It's safe to assume that the culprits would prefer their wrongdoing to go unnoticed, or if noted, not to be traced back to them.

To overcome this roadblock, the crisis communications plan has to convey the message that any employee is going to be worse off by keeping quiet than by talking to the appropriate authorities within the organization. It achieves this, first, by making it clear what type of situations (i.e. crises) must be brought to your attention and, second, by plotting the path by which that information must flow.

So the first thing your crisis communications plan should have is a concise definition of what a crisis is. This should not be an academic or theoretical definition; it must be a practical one designed to grease the wheels of communication. My own definition of a crisis is "anything that could result in adverse publicity."

This should be followed by a brief description of the goals and objectives of the crisis communications plan. Here, too, the aim is to impress upon the organization's employees the absolute necessity of unfettered internal communications and to impress upon middle and senior management their responsibility to cooperate fully with you in the implementation of the plan. You'll have to come up with wording that fits your organization, but I suggest it follow along these lines:

Goal:

To protect the well-being of the ABC Widget Company, its employees, shareholders, customers and the communities in which it operates.

Objectives:

To ensure that the public relations department is informed immediately of any situation that might result in adverse publicity so that appropriate action can be taken, and

To communicate as accurately and as quickly as possible relevant information to our stakeholders, the media and other key publics.

The remainder of the plan describes how that communication is to take place. The details will, of course, vary from organization to organization, but you'll be on the right track if you follow these guidelines:

- Set up lines of communication with each department or division to ensure that you are informed immediately of any crisis.

- Establish a crisis management team. The permanent members should include the CEO or someone authorized to act in his or her place, legal counsel and a senior communications manager. The team would be augmented in any given crisis by the heads of the department or departments directly involved.

- Prepare or assign others to prepare lists of all those inside and outside the company who should be informed when a crisis occurs. This list would obviously include senior management – although they would also likely be informed of the crisis directly – and other designated spokespersons. Others on the list might include your outside legal counsel; relevant municipal, provincial and federal government officials; regulatory authorities; unions; joint-venture partners and, of course, the media. These lists must be complete, containing the name; title; affiliation; mailing and courier addresses; as well as office, home, car and cottage telephone and fax numbers. Some of these lists may have already been compiled by other departments. If so, then the plan should incorporate them.

- Draw up a list of spokespersons. This may include the head of your public affairs or public relations department, the president of the company, or division heads. You want to keep the list as small as possible, since the more voices your organization speaks with, the greater the chances that you will issue conflicting or confusing information. But, if your head office and operations are in different cities, make sure to designate an onsite spokesperson who can deal directly with the local media.

- Ensure that all spokespersons get sufficient media training to handle sharp questions under highly stressful circumstances.

- Establish a firm policy for handling media enquiries. Everyone in the organization should know to whom media calls are to be directed and what to say to persistent reporters who may attempt to pry information out of them.

- List possible crisis situations and outline the appropriate communications responses. This is a "what to do if" exercise. Lacking a crystal ball, you won't predict every possible crisis. But you should be able to cover the bases by identifying specific examples of different types of crises. Then apply all that you know about communications, in general, and media relations, in particular, to figure out when and how your various publics might react and what you should do to best ensure that their reactions will be favourable.

- Identify and assign all tasks that might have to be performed during the various crisis situations you envision. This could include notifying your various publics, arranging for news conferences, writing and distributing news releases or providing meeting rooms and equipment for the media. If your organization operates out of a single office in a major city, the range of possible crises and your response to them would be much more limited and simpler than the crises faced, say, by a mining company with operations in isolated areas or an airline whose planes fly – and may crash – anywhere in the world.

- Distribute relevant parts of the plan to each employee. Most employees should probably get a single sheet of paper containing the crisis definition, the plan's goals and objectives, the policy on direct media calls and any specific tasks that they would be required to perform. The full plan – containing all the detailed crisis scenarios, assigned tasks and complete lists of publics – should be distributed to the permanent members of the crisis management team and deposited in a safe place that will be accessible at any time and under any circumstances.

Putting the Plan Into Effect

If the plan is effective, the public relations department should be hearing about all sorts of minor occurrences within the organization that could result in adverse publicity. These may include the dismissal of an employee suspected of embezzlement, a spate of irate letters from disgruntled customers, a citation for violating environmental regulations or even a media call to the Chief Financial Officer about your earnings forecast for the coming year.

In most cases, you'll file the reports on the occurrences and do nothing. In some cases, you may want to prepare a response in case the story hits the media. In others, you may wish to initiate media coverage or communicate directly with some of your key publics. You may take these actions on your own or consult with the other permanent members of the crisis management team – depending on your evaluation of the gravity of the situation and your authority to deal with it.

On rare occasions, a true disaster will occur. Six people are killed in a factory explosion; toxic fumes are spewed into the air when a transport overturns on the expressway; an extortionist demands $100 million or he'll put shards of glass in the baby food products your company manufactures. What makes these disasters potential PR nightmares is, first, their high degree of newsworthiness and, second, the negative effects that extensive media exposure might have.

When to Inform the Media

When situations of this nature occur, meet immediately with the crisis management team to determine your action plan and your message.

The toughest question you'll have to resolve is whether to inform the media – that is, initiate media coverage – or sit back and wait for the media to come to you. The question is tough because there is a natural instinct to run and hide in the face of unknown and terrible danger – even though running and hiding can be the worst thing you can do. StarKist ran and hid when word got out that a shipment of tuna might have been tainted. The outcome: The plant that produced the tuna (which might, indeed, have been fit for human consumption after all) closed down, throwing more than 200 people out of work. Johnson & Johnson recalled several hundred million dollars worth of Tylenol and communicated willingly and openly with the media when six people died after swallowing poisoned capsules. The outcome: Johnson & Johnson not only recovered its losses, but emerged as an even more profitable company that is now heralded as a stellar corporate citizen.

So when do you initiate media coverage and when do you wait for the media to contact you? If (1) the media will find out anyway, (2) AND they will publish or broadcast the story (3) AND you may not have effective input into the content or tone of the initial story, THEN YOU SHOULD INITIATE MEDIA COVERAGE.

The problem is that you can never be 100 per cent sure. You have to use your best judgement. If the crisis involves a lot of people, some of whom may not be kindly disposed towards you, then assume the media will find out. If the crisis involves the police, then there is little doubt that the media will know of it. As to the likelihood of the media publishing or broadcasting the story, just use your own judgement of its newsworthiness and assume that the media are just as competent as you are in identifying a good story.

Coming to grips with the third criterion – the input that you will have in the initial story – is much more subjective. You'll have to consider the time constraints on the media (the greater the pressure on the reporter, the less likely that he or she will call you or, if you are called, that your comments will be given fair play). You'll have to determine how other publics might react to your crisis and how they might influence the reporter. You must also take into account the reputation you have with the media. If your reputation is good, you have a better chance of getting a fair shake in the initial story. If it's bad, the chances could be slim. To increase them, you should take the initiative and get your message to the media before the media hear it from someone else.

Even if you decide not to initiate media coverage, you must always be available when the media come to you. Refusing to grant interviews, repeating "no comment" to every question, or not returning media calls will invariably have the same result: Media coverage that is more harmful to you than if you spoke to the reporter.

What You Should Tell the Media

And here's what you should say either in your initial news release or in reply to media questions:

- Give the established facts in a clear, straightforward manner, without deceptive euphemisms or jargon.

- Take charge of the situation by saying you will investigate the cause of the occurrence and will use whatever you learn to prevent a recurrence.

- Express sympathy to those who have lost loved ones or property.

What you do next is really guided by the crisis communications plan. But keep these tips in mind:

- Thoroughly brief the designated spokespersons.

- Distribute copies of all news releases to all staff, since it would be far better for employees to hear what's happening from you than to learn about it from the evening news when they get home.

- Make sure the media know who the spokespersons are and where to reach them, and that the spokespersons remain there.

- If the crisis is ongoing, issue a news release whenever a significant development occurs. Otherwise reporters, trying to advance the story at each successive deadline, will tend to go to unauthorized, and perhaps ill-informed or ill-intentioned, sources.

IN BRIEF
Contents of Your Crisis Communications Plan

- Crisis definition.
- Goals and objectives of the plan.
- Internal lines of communication to ensure you're informed of a crises.
- Structure of a crisis management team.
- Detailed lists of individuals to be informed of a crisis.

- List of spokespersons.
- Plan for training designated spokespersons.
- Policy for handling media enquiries.
- Detailed scenarios of most likely crisis situations.
- Identify and assign other tasks.
- Distribute relevant parts of the plan to each employee. ·

When to Initiate Media Coverage

- When the media will find out anyway.
- AND they will publish or broadcast the story.
- AND you may not have effective input into the initial story.

When Not To Initiate Media Coverage

5

Many CEOs, marketing executives and public relations professionals are, by nature, outgoing and gregarious people who thrive on public exposure. They draw satisfaction and strength from their publics in much the same way that entertainers are energized by their audiences. By and large, any organization will be well served by such people. They are often enthusiastic communicators with a genuine liking for people. But there are times when you will have to help them keep their exuberance in check.

Not every issue or event relating to your organization warrants a media program, and not every media program is the same. In deciding how to handle any situation that might arise, ask yourself what you could gain or lose from media exposure.

There can definitely be gains. During the 1980s, John Bullock was practically a household name in Canada, because he had positioned himself as *the* spokesperson on public issues affecting small business. That exposure served a very essential purpose: It built membership in the Canadian Federation of Independent Business. Bullock effectively used the media as a marketing tool.

Speaking out on sundry public issues may have helped Bullock and the CFIB. But it may hurt you. Attacking the government for bad fiscal management or unethical behaviour may earn you a reputation as a fearless crusader, but you may get short shrift the next time you go to your Member of Parliament on a matter that has direct financial bearing on your company.

Thinking Things Through

Here's another situation: A major customer of yours is involved in some kind of public scandal. Because of your business involvement with that company, you know the local media would be sure to print any comments you might make.

Think it through. A supportive comment might put you in the good graces of an important customer, but it might also taint you with the scandal. A negative comment might put you on the side of the angels, but would surely jeopardize a lucrative account. It's a no-win situation, so stay quiet, even if your corporate strategy is to achieve a high public profile.

As the media representative for a large resource company, I was once confronted with just this type of situation. And boy, did I blow it. There was nothing that the reporter could have written, no amount of speculation or innuendo, that would have been worse than the truth. A company with which we were associated was involved, indirectly, in a financial scandal. As a result, my company decided to end the association. It was only natural for the media to call us. We even anticipated it, and planned our response, which was that it was an internal management decision that we would not discuss publicly. We did our crisis management well.

But when the reporter's call came, I didn't follow my own instructions. I found myself wanting to please the reporter – to give him his story. So I tried to explain, as tactfully and as diplomatically as possible, that we ended the association because the other company had been tainted by the scandal. When the story came out, we looked like chumps. I had forgotten one of the first lessons of dealing with the media – how to say "no."

Let the bad media opportunities pass you by and bid them good riddance. That doesn't mean that you should never speak out on controversial issues, but make sure you have a good reason for doing so. And that means making sure that the issue has a bearing on the well-being of your organization.

Warning Signs

There are other times when you should not initiate media coverage, and as a rule the warning signs can easily be spotted. Watch for:

Egos Crying Out   The most important time to not initiate coverage is when your ego cries out for a few inches of ink or a few seconds of tape. Some people just love to see their name in print or hear their words on radio or TV. Ego can be a powerful adversary, so powerful that it can defeat the forces of reason and good judgement.

I'm sure you've seen those "corporate" ads that are dominated by a snapshot of the owner of the company. They're really nothing more than highly transparent exercises in self-promotion. That's what makes them so undesirable. If the people you are trying to reach perceive you as a publicity hound intent primarily on satisfying an inflated ego, you will lose their respect, their trust and perhaps even their business.

The Lure of Sensationalism   Another time to hold the horses is when you find yourself driven by an urge for sensationalism. There are times when you feel your story, as accurately presented, won't get into the media. When that happens, resist the temptation to sensationalize your message. It could backfire on you.

I once wrote a speech for the Chairman of the Canadian Manufacturers' Association that spoke of the need to manage change. To illustrate some of the pitfalls, the speech criticized two pieces of social legislation whose principles the association supported, but whose mechanisms would have been unworkable and counterproductive.

This wasn't news, but it was reality. The speech was very well received by the audience, which consisted of about 200 senior business people, but the media coverage was not that extensive. A PR colleague criticized the speech as lacking media appeal, and he told me it should have supported the two pieces of legislation instead of opposing them. That would have been news, indeed, since it ran counter to the CMA's often-publicized views. The speech would have gotten more ink, but the association, itself, would have lost effectiveness. The media coverage would have frustrated long-term goals, not advanced them.

The media might have loved you for the speech, since it gave them a good story, but the association's members and the government officials the CMA was lobbying on the two pieces of legislation would have utterly lost confidence in the association's pronouncements. And if the association bit into the sensationalist apple once too often, the media would have lost confidence, too.

After all, no one likes to be manipulated, and changing your story to sensationalize it is a crass form of media manipulation. In the end, you would have lost members, lost effectiveness with the politicians and senior government advisors and lost the opportunity for fair media coverage.

You might have created a good story, but you would have paid for it in lost credibility.

So the lesson to learn is: Not every story is a headline grabber. Accept it. Be honest about it to yourselves and to the media. That's important to your credibility. Like the boy that cried wolf, issue too many screaming press releases, and when your truly big story does come along, the media will ignore it.

Negative Information   Also be cautious when the information may be harmful to your organization. In simplistic terms, the thrust of your media relations approach should be to publicize positive developments. I say "in simplistic terms," because there are times when the dissemination of negative information may, in fact, help you achieve your organizational goals. These cases usually involve your credibility – such as the reporting of unfavourable earnings or a not-so-successful fundraising campaign – or your standing as a good corporate citizen – such as the reporting of an environmental spill that may affect significant numbers of people.

You shouldn't hide from the unpleasant parts of life, especially when meeting them head on is not only part of your legal responsibility, but can also make you appear honest, concerned and courageous.

That does not mean, however, that you rush to display all your dirty linen to the media. Many negative things will occur to or within your organization that may be of interest to the media, but which you are under no moral or legal obligation to divulge.

You wouldn't call a press conference to announce, for example, that the US Federal Trade Commission is investigating an accusation of price-fixing against your company. If your stock or debentures trade on any U.S. exchanges, you will have to report that fact in your 10K form. But the existence of the investigation itself is not material – that is, it would not be deemed to affect the value of your stock – and you are under no obligation to report it to the media. So why do it?

Likewise, why would you initiate media coverage of the unforeseen production problems at your new widget plant? That information may be very valuable to your competitors.

But you shouldn't hide from the media, either. Let's say an enterprising reporter learns of the FTC investigation – perhaps through reading your 10K form – and wants to interview someone in the company about it. You could refuse a full interview by simply saying you don't want to discuss the issue while the investigation is continuing. But that won't stop the reporter from writing the story.

Or you could grant an interview, using it as an opportunity to convey an important message to one or more important publics. In deciding how to handle the request for an interview, you would invoke the first step of your crisis communications plan, namely, inform the relevant people within your organization of the request for an interview regarding the price-fixing investigation and outline the stance you recommend be taken, making sure that you clearly identify the key points you would want to make, either in granting or declining the interview request.

Bear in mind, however, that you will frequently be better off by initiating media coverage of negative events when they are of such a nature that the media will find out about them and report them regardless of what you do.

In some cases, what makes an event newsworthy has less to do with the event itself than with the person or organization behind the event. Not every fender bender gets reported in the *Toronto Star*, but if the limousine carrying a government minister piles up on the Don Valley Parkway in the middle of the afternoon rush hour, you can bet the media will be on to the story in a flash.

As the minister's media relations consultant, you would be doing your employer a great service by going to the media with the story, rather than waiting for the media to come to you – perhaps with an array of preconceptions and misconceptions that may find their way into print or be broadcast over radio and television. If the minister was unhurt, make sure the media know that from you right away. Don't wait until you're forced into the position of denying false reports of injury or death. The first impressions are often the strongest and most lasting. Not only will they linger in the face of subsequent denials, but they may cast doubt on the credibility of the denial and the person or organization issuing it.

The sale of major assets, the layoff of a significant portion of your workforce, a senior management shake-up, serious industrial fires or accidents, workplace fatalities, strikes or lockouts, significant environmental damage – you should take charge in this types of situation by informing the media of the "crisis." Your challenge is to ensure that your organization gets as positive media coverage as possible by following the critical path and by implementing your crisis communications plan.

Bafflegab and Fuzzy Thinking   Finally, do not initiate media coverage and do not grant interviews when you don't know what you're talking about. Sounds simple, doesn't it! But the temptation to satisfy the media's quest for information can often be too great to resist. No one wants to appear to be ignorant or ill-informed. It thus takes strength and conviction to refrain from discussing hot topics in which you may not be sufficiently versed, especially when a skillful reporter tries to squeeze information or a good quote out of you by portraying your reluctance as a manifestation of personal inadequacy.

If you don't know how the Finance Minister's idea for a business transfer tax will affect your company or the members of your trade association, don't distribute a news release reacting to his or her announcement just to get your organization's name in the paper. And don't offer an opinion if a reporter calls you for a comment. Just explain that you need to study the concept in greater depth before offering to evaluate it.

IN BRIEF

When Not to Initiate Media Coverage

- When your ego demands media coverage.
- When you feel driven by the urge to sensationalize.
- When the story may be harmful to your organization. (But if the media are going to find out anyway, put your crisis plan into effect.)
- When you don't know what you're talking about.

Who Are   6
The Media And How
Do You Reach Them?

In all, there are more than 4,500 media contact points in Canada.

The media comprise daily newspapers; radio and TV stations; consumer and business newspapers and magazines; and community newspapers. In addition, there are the radio and TV networks, the labyrinth of cable stations, the news syndicates and wire and satellite services.

Added to this are the PR distribution services, such as Canada News-Wire and Canadian Corporate News, where you pay to have your news release distributed word for word as you dictate. What these services carry is not news. They carry promotional material that you pay to have distributed to the media in hopes that it will be printed or broadcast as news.

Media Directories

You do, indeed, need a scorecard to keep track of all the players on the media scene, and the two most popular Canadian scorecards around are the Matthews directories and Bowdens Media Directory. In the past, I felt I needed both directories in my work as a media relations consultant, since each directory had major flaws or omissions. However, these directories operate in a highly competitive environment, and each has undergone significant improvements in recent years. So if you've been using one directory for a while and are sticking to it out of habit, you may benefit from a review of what each has to offer.

Currency Bowdens, which is packaged in a single loose-leaf binder, updates half of the directory every two months. Each section is thus updated every four months, or three times a year. The complete Matthews list comes in three separately bound volumes.

The Matthews Media Directory, which contains the list of daily newspapers, radio and TV stations, business publications, networks, publishers and news services, is updated three times a year. The Matthews CATV Directory, which lists cable systems, and the Matthews CCE Directory, which lists community newspapers, consumer magazines and ethnic media, are each updated twice a year.

Completeness   Bowdens lists Members of Parliament and members of the federal cabinet, which Matthews does not. Aside from this, when it comes to the degree of information and the way in which it is presented, Matthews either equals or exceeds Bowdens on all fronts.

This wasn't the case when *Managing the Media* was first published in 1989, but since then Matthews was purchased by Canadian Corporate News, which critically examined the publication and eliminated virtually all the deficiencies. Matthews caught up to Bowdens by including sections on community newspapers and ethnic media; Matthews, which used to suffer from poor indexing, has now surpassed Bowdens by having an index of each person and media outlet listed in the directory; and overall, Matthews contains more media listings and more contact people per listing.

The one remaining significant difference is cost. A subscription to Bowdens is $200 per year, compared with $370 per year for all three of the Matthews directories. Matthews does, however, sell each of the three directories separately.

The Canadian Media

Type of Medium	Quantity
Daily newspapers	114
Radio stations	622
Television stations	118
Business publications	602
Consumer publications	624
Community newspapers	1,149
Cable TV stations	850
News, satellite and wire services	28
Radio and television networks	32
Syndicated features and newspaper services	8
Ethnic press	432
Total	4,579

What each directory will tell you is that there are thousands of media people in Canada. How to relate effectively to them is the essence of this book.

Compiling a Media List

Once you've identified the publics you want to reach, you have to identify the specific media to carry your message. To do this most effectively, I strongly recommend that you establish and maintain your own media list culled from either Bowdens or Matthews or both.

The list should include the general media in the geographic areas where your major publics work or live, as well as any business, trade or consumer publications that cover your activities.

It should also contain the names, titles and phone numbers of the relevant editors and reporters at each media outlet. My Macintosh, for example, contains the names of hundreds of journalists, with each listing coded so that I can easily retrieve the names, addresses and phone numbers of virtually any category of editor and writer working for any category of newspaper, radio and TV station, network or news service.

It's easier to make up a core list and update it regularly, than to start from scratch every time you want to send something out. And if you don't want to do the work yourself, you can buy media lists from Bowdens, Matthews or firms specializing in such lists, which will tailor a media list to your exact specifications.

Selecting the Right Media

There are times when you will want to blanket the media with your story, with the only limitations being the amount of money you want to spend on media distribution and the time you have to prepare a sufficient number of media kits.

For some stories, however, you may want to be selective in the publics you want to reach. Let's say, for example, that your smelter and refinery haven't been able to meet the standards for high-grade copper cathode. Well, at long last, you've solved the problem and you want to get the word out. Your most important public consists of your customers and potential customers who have expressed concern about the quality of your product. In this case, you would focus your media program on the technical publications read most extensively by your existing and potential customers. You might also want to use the business media to tell your good news to the investment community – but only if the difficulty you had with the quality of your copper cathode had been depressing the value of your company's shares. If not, you might not want to advertise the fact that you actually had a problem in the first place.

The wire services, major dailies and radio and TV networks are obvious media for most of your communications initiatives. But look deeper. If you're a mining company planning to begin exploration near, say, Manitoulin Island, you'd do well to know the local media. You can bet the cottagers and many of the locals won't be happy about your plans. Knowing how to get your viewpoint in the Manitoulin *Expositor* could be decisive.

The vertical media can also be vital to your success. There are newspapers and magazines out there devoted to supplying virtually every industry with technical or marketing information. Many of them are well-read, but operate on shoestring budgets with small editorial staffs. As a result, they must get most of their news and feature articles directly from industry sources. Get a rundown of their editorial lineups for the coming year and arrange to supply them with relevant articles. You'll have a ready-made opportunity to get an article published over which you have almost complete control.

Many newspapers (and radio stations) will run columns that contain useful information about various products and services – tips on taxes, buying a house, maintaining your car. The more than 900 Canadian community newspapers are an excellent and receptive medium for reaching millions of households with news features or how-to articles. These are known as sponsored editorials, and differ from advertising copy or the standard news releases in that they do not specifically or overtly promote a particular product or company. Instead, they convey helpful or interesting information which is only obliquely linked to an organization, through a single mention of the organization in the copy or an identity tag in the byline, for example.

Media Distribution Methods

There are many ways to get your story to the media. A particular media program might use just one or a combination of several of these means of communication. Which you choose will depend on the media you want to reach, the nature and quantity of the material you want the media to have, your timing and your budget.

By phone   You could read the story over the phone. This is the most personal way to give your release, and I suppose it does afford the journalist the opportunity to ask questions. But unless you have a pretty good reason, don't call up your favourite journalist every time you want to make an announcement. You'll just make a nuisance of yourself.

There are times, however, when phoning in your news release is the only way to get it into the hands of selected media. Shortly after becoming Vice-President, Public Affairs for Kidd Creek Mines, I visited the newspaper, television station and the handful of radio stations in Timmins, where the company has its mines and processing plants. Kidd Creek was the largest single employer in the region and whatever affected the company affected the community, so I wanted to get to know the media first hand and I wanted them to get to know me.

I discovered, however, that no mechanism had ever been set up for getting the company's news to the Timmins media. We used Canada News-Wire to distribute our news releases around the country, but at that time the local media didn't subscribe to Canada News-Wire. What's more, none had fax or telex machines. So, through inadvertence, the company had been shutting out one of its most important media outlets. The solution was to have the company's local operations hand-deliver all routine news releases and for my office in Toronto to telephone all important releases to each of the media outlets.

By mail   The least expensive way to get your news releases and support material to a reporter or editor is by mail. You also have flexibility – you can put whatever you want in the package, whether it is a full-fledged Media Information Kit or merely a few sheets of paper.

The obvious drawback, however, is time. Delivery will not only take several days, but you cannot ensure that the various media will receive your material simultaneously. That's all right for weekly or monthly publications, but not the daily media, which need important news quickly.

So if your material is of a timeless nature, if your information kits are intended to generate media interest in an upcoming event or to set up interviews, or if you are targeting periodicals as opposed to the daily media, then using Canada Post is probably your best bet.

You don't have to do you own mailing. You can buy into any of several news distribution services that will mail your copy to any number of Canadian media points. News Canada, which has been around since 1981, will typeset your story in a standard font and column-width and mail it monthly, along with hundreds of other articles, to Canada's extensive network of community and daily newspapers. The fees vary by space and frequency. According to the 1994 rates, a one-time insertion of a 500-word article, for example, will cost $1,000 to typeset and distribute. If you want to send 52 articles of 250 words each (an average of 4.3 articles per monthly mailing), the annual fee would be $18,000. At no extra charge, News Canada will monitor the various newspapers and send you clippings of your articles.

For a more modest fee, you can include your news release in packets mailed regularly by the various provincial community newspaper associations. Or you can compile your own customized media list and do your own mailing. This would enable you to send personalized letters or memos addressed by name to the specific editors and writers you want to reach.

By courier   Sending your material by courier combines the advantages of using the mails with speed. It is the fastest way to distribute full Media Information Kits. If you're trying to reach a large number of media points, the drawback, of course, is cost. But if you want to reach a relatively select group of media within your geographic area, the cost is actually quite small – just a few dollars per parcel.

By PR Wire   PR wires distribute news releases in much the same way that a wire service like the Canadian Press distributes news. The difference is that you pay the PR wire to transmit your information exactly as you've prepared it to the newsrooms of the nation, while a wire service is a legitimate news operation supplying finished news copy to the print and broadcast media. In the case of the PR wire, you are the client. In the case of the news agency, the newspaper is the client. You have no guarantee that a newspaper or television or radio station will use the release you send over a PR wire, just as you have no guarantee that the release will be used if you send it by mail or courier.

For getting news releases into the highest number of newsrooms simultaneously and in the shortest amount of time, nothing beats Canada News-Wire. But you pay for the privilege. Canada

News-Wire is the most comprehensive media distribution network in Canada – with a series of different "networks" so you can also target the media you want to reach – and is also the most expensive. For an additional fee, Canada News-Wire can have your release distributed to US media points through an arrangement with its American counterpart, PR News Wire.

Canada News-Wire also distributes news releases to more than 70 brokerage houses across the country as well as to the nation's four stock exchanges, which meets any Canadian disclosure requirements you might have. In addition, all news releases distributed by the service are fed into Infomart and Globe Information Services, two of Canada's most extensive media data bases, and into Canquote, a database used by the investment community.

Canadian Corporate News, another PR wire, which was founded in 1983, is an aggressive rival to Canada News-Wire. Its forte is distribution of news releases to the investment community, hitting about 200 brokerage houses across Canada. Like Canada News-Wire, its news releases are entered into the Canquote system. And also like Canada News-Wire, Canadian Corporate News meets the timely disclosure requirements of the Canadian and US stock exchanges and security commissions. Canadian Corporate News, however, reaches far fewer media points on its wire than Canada News-Wire, so as a purely media distribution network it is less effective.

Canadian Corporate News, however, charges considerably less than Canada News-Wire, and if you only care about reaching the larger media outlets, CCN would be the better choice.

The major drawback of these services, of course, is the impossibility of distributing over the wire the brochures and other printed material that you might want to include in your Media Information Kits.

By fax   Virtually all Canadian dailies and radio and TV stations now have fax machines, and transmitting your news release over fax is cheaper than PR wires or couriers. It has three added advantages over the PR wires.

First, your copy does not have to be retyped for transmission, thus eliminating the possibility of error (although, if you have the equipment, it is possible to feed your news release directly from your computer to Canada News-Wire's computer). Second, the material is an exact (albeit black and white) replica of your original, which means it goes in the format you want and on the letterhead you want. Third, you can modify the material to suit different media or you can address your news release or editor's note to a particular person.

There are, however, certain disadvantages. The receiving fax machine might be busy, necessitating redialing, just as with any busy telephone signal. You will not get exactly simultaneous delivery. Even sophisticated fax machines that can transmit simultaneously over several hundred fax lines can't break through a busy signal or send to a machine that's out of paper – so there could be a gap of up to two or three hours from the time the message is transmitted to the first and last points on your media list. You can overcome this handicap by scheduling the most important or most competitive media first. Finally, unsolicited faxes are becoming a nuisance, and many media would simply prefer that you send your news release by some other means. Of course, if it's really newsworthy, they would want your news release no matter how it's sent – as long as it gets there quickly. And individual reporters, even on large newspapers, may want to get your news release addressed to them personally by fax, even if you are also sending it on one of the PR wires. These arrangements should, however, be made ahead of time.

At a news conference   News conferences can be valuable tools, if used sparingly and intelligently. Their greatest advantage is that they establish direct contact with several reporters at once. They are therefore often the first thing that executives think of when they want to get something across to the media.

But that's not always the best idea. News conferences are demanding, of you and especially of the media. None of the distribution techniques discussed so far demands the time or attention of the media; they all allow the individual editor and reporter to deal with the story when and as they want to. The news conference, on the other hand, requires a strong commitment to the story by the editor and reporter before they know exactly what they're getting.

There are times, though, when you should call a news conference. One is when you want to demonstrate a new product or service. If that's the case, make sure you bring along something to demonstrate. A colleague once told me of a news conference that failed because the bank that had arranged it to announce the introduction of a new kind of automated teller machine didn't bother to bring one along so the media could see, describe and film it in action. There's not much point in dragging the media to a news conference just to listen to a couple of talking heads. They could have gotten the information from a news release.

You should, however, hold a news conference when you've got a celebrity to show off. Here a talking head is your selling point, especially for radio or television.

You might have no alternative to holding a news conference when several people or organizations are involved in the news issue to be released to the media, and each participant wants to tell a different aspect of the story, and regular news conferences or briefings may be the most effective way to maintain control of the flow of information during a drawn-out crisis situation.

If your story does not fall into any of the foregoing categories, you should call a news conference only if:

- The story is of great media interest and

- It has a strong time element so that each news outlet will want to publish or broadcast the story as soon as possible because of competition with other news outlets and

- The story requires contact with the media, perhaps because it is so complex that you cannot expect to answer foreseeable questions in a reasonably compact Media Information Kit, or there are photo or video opportunities.

Not calling a news conference for a story that meets all three criteria would put the media at a great disadvantage. To be complete, your media kit would likely be so large and complicated that it would take the reporters too long to glean the relevant information from it. As a result, you would probably get so many enquiries that you'd be on the phone for hours on end, with most reporters getting through to you too late for their deadlines.

If, however, the story is of only limited news value, then the media will be satisfied with a brief news release. If the story is a timely and newsworthy one, but can be easily grasped and simply told, you can also get your message across effectively in the standard news release and fact sheets that make up most Media Information Kits. Some reporters may still have questions, but there won't be so many that you wouldn't be able to answer them rapidly and within the deadline requirements of all interested reporters. Remember, when reporters come to news conferences, they want a major story. If you disappoint them once, you may not get a second chance.

If you do call a news conference, you should be aware of two major drawbacks. One is that it is often difficult to get all the media together at one time. Assignments cannot always be made in advance, especially for the broadcast media, and reporters may be called away on fast-breaking stories. Another is that you could lose control. Be too open or indiscreet with a single reporter, and your mistake might appear only once. Do that in a news conference and all the media may report it. Let one reporter get you off your main point, and that could influence the coverage you get from the other media representatives at the news conference.

If after all this you decide to hold a news conference, know what you're doing.

- Make sure the room is big enough to accommodate camera operators, lighting, TV and radio interviewers and the print media. Too often, the print reporters get in the way of the cameras and the TV or radio reporters, or the cameras and lights create a barrier between the print reporters and the person holding the press conference.

- Make an opening statement before inviting questions. After all, what you want to say is the reason for your calling the news conference, and you've got to give the reporters something upon which to base their questions. Conversely, always allow questions. If you're not prepared for media probing, don't hold a news conference.

- Always distribute a Media Information Kit. This will give the reporters reference material when writing their stories back in the newsroom. And if you distributed a Media Information Kit prior to the news conference, don't assume the reporter who shows up will have ever seen it. Have plenty of copies on hand.

- Serve coffee, tea, juice and light pastries. It's not only thoughtful, it gives you a good opportunity to chat informally with the media before the news conference begins and possibly afterwards as well, if the reporters are not on deadline and don't have another story to cover.

By one-on-one interviews   My personal preference is to avoid news conferences whenever possible. I prefer one-on-one interviews. They will give you direct and personal contact with the media and will limit any damage in the event you lose control. You may mishandle the interview with one newspaper, but you will also learn from that mistake when meeting with another paper later in the day.

There are two important caveats, however.

One is time and energy. You'll need both. It will take a lot of your time and energy to set up interviews, and it will demand the time and energy of the person giving the interviews.

Two is irritation. Kenneth Kidd, then a business writer for the *Toronto Star*, once aired his gripes about pushy publicists. Sharing top honours with the number of news releases that landed on his desk every day were the number of phone calls he got every day.

He writes of news releases, "Often, they are supported by phone calls from the publicist – 'We will be sending you . . .' 'Have you received . . .?' 'What do you think . . .?' 'Will you be attending . . .?' 'Can I call you again, just to make sure?'

"Multiply this process by the number of press releases, and the answer can be half a day's worth of general irritation."

I've been guilty of this transgression, and I'm sure most other media relations people have, too. But I wouldn't let Kidd's frustration intimidate you, either.

There are times when you should call the media to set up interviews. Budget night is a good example. If you believe your opinions are newsworthy, you might call the TV networks or other selected media, to announce your availability for a reaction to the budget speech and, if they're interested, to make arrangements as to where and when to meet. This helps both you and them. Budget night can be pretty hectic, with the halls of Parliament cluttered with a maniacal maze of TV cables and crazed reporters. In these situations, calling beforehand to set up interviews has worked out well for the major industry associations and public affairs organizations.

You would also be justified in calling the media to set up interviews on the basis of material you had already sent them. I had great success several years ago in Ottawa with a brochure I had produced on the strides Falconbridge had made in reducing its sulphur dioxide emissions. I sent a copy of the brochure to the media along with a news release and covering letter saying I'd be in Ottawa for interviews on two given days. I followed this up with phone calls asking whether they'd received the material, had any questions or would like to interview me when I was in town. The *Citizen*, as well as half a dozen radio and TV stations, took me up on the offer.

This technique also worked out quite well a few years ago for the Appraisal Institute of Canada. The president that year was a fellow from New Brunswick and, as every president does at the beginning of his two-year term, he toured the country to meet with the various branches and get some media coverage along the way. During his two days in Toronto, we had arranged more than a dozen interviews for him, which led to two television appearances, several lengthy radio interviews, a stint on a 90-minute talk show, full-length articles in the *Financial Post*, the *Star* and the *Globe and Mail*, and a TV feature in which the reporter had the president appraise the value of my house.

One strong note of caution: Don't overdo it. Nine out of 10 stories – and that's a conservative estimate – rate no more than a brief news release to be mailed to the media or transmitted on a public relations news wire. Of the remaining stories, if you're not sure whether they are sufficiently newsworthy to call the media about interviews, let the media decide for themselves. Simply append a note to the news release saying that so-and-so will be available for in-person or telephone interviews at such-and-such place and time, and let it go at that.

IN BRIEF
Getting Your Story to the Media

1. Give the story over the phone.
    + Excellent way to target the media.
    + May be the only way to reach a particular news outlet.
    – Time-consuming, especially for the reporter or editor.
2. Send it through the mail.
    + Least expensive way to distribute the media kit.
    + Excellent way to target the media.
    + Good technique when publicizing upcoming event.
    – Will take several days.
    – No assurance of simultaneous delivery.
3. Send it by courier.
    + Fastest way to distribute full Media Information Kit.
    + Excellent way to target the media.
    – Expensive to use.
    – No assurance of simultaneous delivery.
4. Transmit it on Canada News-Wire or Canadian Corporate News.
    + Fastest way to reach most media.
    + Distribution can be targeted by province and region.

+ Distribution is simultaneous.
- Expensive to use.
- Cannot distribute printed material.

5. Transmit it by fax.
   + Fast way to reach most media.
   + Reasonably inexpensive.
   + Excellent way to target the media.
   - No assurance of simultaneous delivery.
   - May irritate the media.

6. Call a news conference.
   + Establishes direct contact with several reporters at once.
   - Difficult to assemble all the media at one time.
   - Risk of losing control over media coverage.

7. Arrange interviews with individual reporters.
   + Establishes direct contact with reporter.
   + Each reporter can develop own story idea.
   + Limited damage if you lose control over the interview.
   - Time-consuming.

Nine General Rules   7
For Dealing
With The Media

I've formulated nine general rules to follow when dealing with the media. Use them and you will reap the rewards.

1. Give relevant facts quickly

Come up with the relevant facts quickly. You'll make the reporter's job that much easier and you'll earn his or her gratitude and respect. That is more likely to result in a favourable story about you than a gruff "no comment," a door slammed in the face or a tardy response that misses the reporter's deadline.

The next time your boss complains that the newspaper misinterpreted an event, didn't include a vitally important fact or didn't present the views of your company or organization fairly, was it because you didn't return the reporter's phone call? And the next time you get miffed because your organization's opinion on a relevant, burning issue wasn't sought by the media, could it have been because your organization is known for its slackness in replying to media enquiries?

In my day as a business reporter for the *Toronto Star*, I cultivated those PR people who quickly met my need for fast and accurate information. When Ontario passed new condominium legislation, I merely gave one of these fellows a call and within 15 minutes he set up interviews with three of the province's major developers. I had a good reaction story, and the PR guy got some positive publicity for his clients.

2. Say "no" if necessary

Be firm but courteous, if you have to say no. Some information is confidential and the public simply has no right to have it. If that's the case, don't beat around the bush. Coca-Cola isn't coy about not divulging its formula, and neither should you be coy about not giving out proprietary information. But don't be judgmental. A brief explanation that the company doesn't want to disclose certain information for competitive reasons, for example, will be much more effective than a curt "that's none of your business." And don't chastise the reporter for asking. The media have as much right to ask as you have not to answer.

Of course, there are reporters who won't take "no" for an answer, which is not a bad trait for someone who makes his living by prying secrets loose from the unwary. But your living may well depend on not telling secrets, so you'd better learn how to keep them from insistent reporters. Above all, don't play 20 questions. If the unit cost of producing a widget in your new factory is sensitive competitive information that the company wants to keep confidential, don't let the reporter rattle you into inadvertently giving that information.

"Give me a ballpark figure," the reporter might plead. "Is it less than $100 per unit?"

"As I said," you reply, "that's sensitive competitive information that we don't divulge."

"Well," inveigles the reporter, "the widgets retail for $250 each. Given normal markups I would estimate the production cost at $125."

"As I said," you reply calmly and patiently, "that's sensitive competitive information that we don't divulge."

"I see," says the reporter, his voice betraying signs of impatience. "I'll have to write something, and if you don't give me the information I'll have to just go with what I have."

"As I said," you reply yet again in that same calm and patient voice, "that's sensitive competitive information that we don't divulge."

At this point, you're starting to get nervous. What if the reporter uses incorrect information? What if the reporter will express his frustration by writing something nasty about me or my company? To protect the company and myself, perhaps I should give just a little hint of the unit cost?

Forget it. Chances are the reporter was bluffing when he threatened to use unsubstantiated information. But even if he does include that figure in his story, the dangers are still less than if you had divulged confidential information. Unless the reporter lied and attributed his made-up figure to you, your competitors and customers will still not know your cost of production. That is, after all, your reason for not divulging the information in the first place. And if the reporters are going to lie, it doesn't really matter what you tell them, so you haven't lost anything by keeping your mouth shut.

As far as reporters getting even with you by printing something nasty, that, too, is highly unlikely. You do, however, increase the odds by being nasty and abusive yourself. Conversely, of course, you reduce the odds by being calm and courteous.

As far as compromising by hinting at the truth, all you'll really accomplish is losing the respect of the reporter. No one respects a snitch.

I've never been burned by saying "no" when saying "no" was appropriate. I recall one recent exchange with a reporter who was trying to pry some number or other out of me. She asked me the question in seven different ways, but to each question I gave the same answer. I tried to keep cool as I sensed her rising anger, but she was just putting on an act. As soon as she realized that she wasn't going to get the tidbit of information, she dropped her pretence and remarked lightheartedly, "Well, Ed, you can't blame me for trying."

I got a frantic call one day from the president of a large Canadian company who said, "I'm giving an interview to the *Globe*, and I need your help." He felt comfortable generally about the topic of the interview, but was concerned that the reporter would ask him about one particular bit of information that he did not want to give out. He wanted my advice on how to deal with this problem.

So I told him to say "no" and explain why, and to be prepared for a series of questions, each phrased a bit differently from the other, and simply to give the same answer to each.

"Great," he said, much relieved, and marched off to the interview.

Sure enough, the next day in the *Globe* the president was quoted saying exactly what he did not want to say. When I asked him why, he said, "I did what you said, but after a while the reporter got really annoyed. 'You keep skirting the issue,' she told me. 'Now I want a straight answer.' I had no choice, I had to give her the information."

"The hell you did," I said. "You didn't have to give that information after her last demand, just as you didn't have to give it in reply to her first, second, third, fourth or fifth question. All she did was steer you away from your agenda and into her own. Your answer to her demand for a 'straight answer' should have been the same as the answer you had given all along – 'that information is confidential.' "

3. Nothing is off the record

There is no such thing as "off the record". Everything you say becomes part of the public record and could be used by the reporter.

4. Don't play favourites

Be fair. Don't play favourites. If you're planning to make an announcement, make sure that all the media that might be interested get the story and get it as simultaneously as possible. Competing media often judge their own performance on how quickly they break a story. Sometimes this is measured in days, sometimes in hours, sometimes in minutes.

As the Reuters correspondent in Denmark, I'd rush like crazy to get an important story on the wire just two or three minutes ahead of UPI, the Associated Press or AFP. Somewhere, there's a newspaper or radio or TV station that's on deadline, and the first version of a story to land on the editor's desk is likely to be the one that's used.

Your job is not to get caught up in the competition among the various media. If you do, you'll be loved by those you favour, despised by those you don't and respected by none of them. So if a reporter asks for an early break of your quarterly earnings, explain your policy of fairness and say no. This doesn't mean, however, that you don't reward an enterprising reporter who may want to delve into newsworthy areas that other, less energetic reporters may have ignored.

The rules of thumb on fairness are simple:
- If the information requested is confidential, say so.
- If the information is going to be released at an announced time and place, don't give it out earlier to some and not to others.
- If the information is already available to anyone who bothers to enquire, give it out when asked.

There's an important corollary to this rule: Keep your conversations with reporters confidential. If, through diligence and perseverance, one paper manages to dig up a good exclusive about your organization, don't spill the beans to the other paper in town.

5. Probe tactfully

Probe, especially when you get unsolicited media enquiries. You want to know what kind of story the reporter is working on both to prevent damaging references to your organization and to seek out opportunities for getting across some of your positive messages. How to probe can be tricky. You don't want to alienate the reporter by appearing to criticize his or her professionalism or to censor what the reporter may write. The tone of your questions should be helpful, not accusatory.

Not too long ago, a reporter called me for information about one of my clients. He wanted certain facts about the company's activities. I didn't know the reporter personally, but it didn't take long on the phone for me to realize that he had already made up his mind about a highly controversial issue, and was intent on doing a hatchet job on my client.

I had a choice. I could have refused to answer his questions. After all, why help the enemy? But I knew that this would not stop the story; it would merely ensure that my client's point of view would be excluded. So I took another tack. I was helpful. I enquired whether the information I had given was sufficient. I was honest and direct about not having a couple of facts at my disposal, then I kept my promise to get the required information to him as quickly as possible.

And I probed — both for the content of the story the reporter was preparing and for the reporter's biases. I learned something vital — the reporter was told by a source he wouldn't reveal that the company was hedging on quality to increase production.

The reporter said he had tried to reach the company's president for the past two days, but his calls were not returned. It was obvious to me and probably to the reporter as well that the president was hiding. He didn't want to talk to an obviously antagonistic journalist.

As soon as I got off the phone with the reporter, I got hold of the president with one firm bit of advice: Return that call and set the record straight. This he did, giving the reporter an opportunity to question him about the company's quality control and giving the president an opportunity to state unequivocally that the unnamed source's information was wrong.

Of course, there are no guarantees that any reporter will either report your side of the story, or report it accurately. But that's where your skills in media relations come in – not to guarantee success, but to maximize your chances of success.

6. Be respectful and polite

Develop a positive attitude when dealing with the media. That means getting down to the basics of proper social and business behaviour. Be respectful and polite, just as you would to a valued customer, employee or outside consultant. It's like catching flies with honey. It's knowing that people are more likely to treat you fairly when you treat them fairly. Again, there are no guarantees. You're just trying to push the odds a little bit more in your favour, just as Blue Jays Manager Cito Gaston does when he platoons a left-handed batter against a right-handed pitcher.

There's no doubt about it – sooner or later a reporter is going to write or say something that'll push you over the edge. It has happened to my colleagues and it has happened to me. Most of the time, I've been able to hold myself in check, but there has also been the odd time when I, too, got angry and mouthed off. And every time I did, I've come to regret it. The fact is, if you lose your temper, it's going to be your angry words, your blustering and your loss of control that will be reported or broadcast – not the reporter's provocation. The public will not know that the reporter was being snide, sarcastic, rude, pushy or just plain stupid. They will know only that you were abusive and uncommunicative.

7. Get to know key reporters

Get to know the key reporters who cover your organization's activities. You don't have to become bosom buddies; acquaintanceship can do just fine.

Invite reporters, either individually or in groups, to your office or plant for a chat and a tour. Introduce them to your senior staff.

Ask reporters what kinds of stories they are interested in. You'll pick up invaluable tips on how to present your story to them and you'll probably pick up a lot of story ideas as well.

Taking a reporter or editor out to lunch may be helpful to both of you, if you keep it on a businesslike basis. Reporters may also want to take you to lunch. After all, they want sources of information as much as you want outlets for information. Media contacts have often asked me for the names of my clients so they would know who to call if an occasion ever arose when they needed an authoritative source.

But beware. You can do yourself a lot of damage by "wining and dining" the media. Some reporters may view it as a form of bribery – of these, some may be open to the suggestion and you might proceed at your own risk, but others will resent it as an attack on their professionalism and integrity. I knew one very sensitive reporter who, after the public relations person jokingly implied that he attended the annual dinner merely to take advantage of a "freebie," refused to go to any functions held by that particular industry association. So be careful.

8. Understand how the media work

Know the deadlines and understand the other restraints under which the media operate.

The most pressing restraint facing a journalist is, in fact, the deadline. When the deadline passes, your information is no longer news. So when the business reporter for your local TV station calls you at three in the afternoon for an interview with your resident expert on the question of equal pay for work of equal value, treat the request with some urgency. The reporter probably has his back against the wall. He needs some pithy quotes for the six o'clock news and so far he's come up dry. So if you come up with the goods – or at least make a good showing – you'll earn his gratitude. The next time he needs an informed comment, he'll likely think of you first. And the next time you've got a potential news item you want covered, he'll be more likely to do the story.

Another restraint is the editor. "Beat" reporters – those who report on specific subjects – generally plan their own assignments, usually after consultation with their editor. Otherwise, assignments usually originate with the editors, and the reporter who gets an assignment may not be familiar with your organization or the issue at hand. You may be asked what you regard as stupid or irrelevant questions. Don't lose patience. After all, if the reporter doesn't understand the issues or the facts, how do you expect him to write about them accurately or fairly?

The few minutes you spend explaining the situation to a reporter may save you hours of aggravation later on. But keep your explanations simple, and to the point. The more you wander off track or the more complex you make the issue, the greater the chance the reporter will get it wrong.

TV crews have special needs. All a newspaper reporter needs is a pen and pad. The surroundings really don't matter much. But a TV crew needs space, proper lighting, an attractive background, time to set up equipment and an environment that's free of noise. Anticipate these needs and be accommodating. Don't set up a television interview along a busy corridor adjacent to the typing pool.

9. Don't blame reporters

Don't blame the reporter for something he or she didn't do. The headline may be misleading, but it's not the reporter's fault. The reporter didn't write it. A copy editor did, most likely under extremely tense deadline pressure.

You're angry because your interview didn't get in the paper. The reporter may have written it, but there wasn't enough available space that day. The decision to hold your interview was made by a news editor, not the reporter.

The same goes for great quotes or important facts you gave the reporter. He may have included them in his article, but the story may have been edited down to fit into limited space. And all that goes double for the broadcast media, where every day, hundreds of minutes of tape or film must be edited down to fit into a half-hour news program.

This doesn't mean that you will let things pass, merely because the error might not have been the reporter's fault. If a story was factually incorrect, biased or unbalanced, the record should be set straight. It's just that you should go about it in the right way – and that means not blaming reporters for something they didn't do.

The corollary of this is that you should rarely, if ever, cast blame. Your goal is not to punish an errant reporter or editor, it's to get the media to tell your story the way you want it told. Management at the newspaper or the radio and TV news departments determine who should be reprimanded for shoddy reporting.

Following these rules will help you become a valuable source of reliable information for the media. This won't guarantee that the media will not publish or broadcast stories critical of your organization, but it will increase the chances that whatever is published or broadcast will be balanced. And it will make it easier for you to interest a reporter in a story you would like to see covered.

IN BRIEF

Nine Rules: The "Do's" and "Don'ts" of Dealing with the Media

1. Come up with the relevant facts quickly.
2. Say "no" if you have to, but be firm, courteous and direct.
3. Don't say anything you don't want reported. There is no such thing as "off the record."
4. Don't play favourites with the media.
5. Probe tactfully for a reporter's intentions and biases.
6. Have a positive attitude and be respectful and polite.
7. Get to know key reporters.
8. Understand the restraints under which the media operate.
9. Don't blame reporters for something they didn't do.

Interviews 8

Studies have shown that making a public presentation is, for humanity as a whole, more stressful than marriage, divorce, getting fired or paying taxes. And giving a media interview is, arguably, the most stressful form of public presentation. Mighty corporate leaders who have successfully clawed their way to the executive washroom are reduced to fear and trembling by the media. Managers who jump at the chance to make a luncheon speech at the local Rotary Club will cower at the prospect of meeting a reporter face-to-face.

Why? Most likely because when you make a presentation, you are communicating directly with your audience. When you give an interview, the reporter stands between you and your audience, leaving your words and thoughts vulnerable to distortion. But with the proper training and preparation, no one need fear the outcome of a media interview. That's not to say you won't be nervous. Even the most accomplished and successful actors get stage fright. And you will, too. But those same actors overcome their fear and parade confidently onto the stage or before the camera because they have an ingrained confidence in their ability to perform well. You should, too.

Personally, I like to feel a little nervous before an interview. That nervousness tells me that my adrenalin is flowing, that my body and mind are getting mobilized for the coming campaign. It's when I'm not a little nervous that I get worried – worried that I might be getting a bit too complacent.

Mention the word interview, and most people imagine a formal exchange between reporter and subject. The reporter's pencil is poised, the lights are blazing and the camera's rolling. There's comfort in that image. You know that your words are about to be recorded for posterity, or at least for immediate consumption on the nightly news. Your mind and body are alert.

That's fine, as far as it goes, which, often, is not far enough. The converse to that scenario is that your mind and body are not on alert when the pencil is still tucked in the reporter's breast pocket and you believe you're merely having a casual conversation, in person or over the phone, with a reporter.

There are many kinds of interviews, and the formal question and answer variety is only one of them. If a reporter asks you the time of day as you step off the elevator, that's an interview. When the reporter rushes up to you after the annual meeting for a clarification of a point you raised in your address to the shareholders, that's an interview. And when a reporter begins a conversation with a disparaging remark about a government minister in hopes of getting your reaction, that, too, is an interview.

In fact, everything you say to a reporter under any circumstances is an interview. Some of you may recall an episode that occurred a few years ago. A federal minister was giving a taped interview to be broadcast later that day. At one point, they took a break, but the camera was still rolling. The reporter and the minister relaxed and engaged in a bit of small talk while waiting for the interview to resume. "So tell me," the reporter asked innocently, "you've told me what you want the public to know, but what do you really think?"

The minister, believing that this was just a friendly little chat between two buddies, dutifully told the reporter what he really did think. And guess what? When the interview was aired that evening, the minister's formal lies and informal truths were broadcast one after the other.

"Foul," cried the minister, "my off-the-cuff remarks were not part of the interview and should not have been aired."

Bull! Everything you say to a reporter constitutes an interview – and don't ever forget it.

How Reporters Work

We are all saddled with prejudices and myths about reporters, and like most prejudices, there's a bit of truth to them. That's what makes them so dangerous and so difficult to shed.

Aside from the stereotype of the reporter as ill-groomed and ill-clothed, one of the most persistent perceptions of your local reporter is that he or she is either out to get a story, no matter whose toes are trampled, or is an unprincipled sensationalist who wants to nail you to the cross.

You can be sure that some of them will fit one of those descriptions because there are always a few people in any large group who are distrustful, prejudiced, vindictive or simply too limited to see two sides of a question.

But most reporters are not out to get you. They're out to get a legitimate story. They need facts, and their livelihood depends on getting them right and getting them fast.

It doesn't take much to figure out which type of reporter you'd rather deal with. But you don't always have a choice. So deal with both types in the same way.

Arranging Media Interviews

If you feel that your story rates a special effort to arrange interviews, follow this six-point plan:

1. Establish your news peg. Your "story" and your "news peg" may be one and the same. But they may be different. In the case of the Appraisal Institute, the story, which frankly wasn't worth very much, was that the president was in town. We couldn't sell that to the media. So we looked for something that the president could say or do that would be newsworthy. In the end, we decided he should issue a statement on how to make housing more affordable for the first-time buyer. That was our news peg.

2. Write a news release based on your news peg.

3. Assemble a Media Information Kit, containing the news release, background information on your organization, a biographical sketch and photograph of the person seeking the interview, and a covering letter to editors explaining the significance of the person and what he has to say and inviting interviews.

4. Anticipate how many interviews you might have, and set aside sufficient time for them.

5. Distribute the Media Information Kit to your selected media list so it arrives about a week before you want the interviews.

6. After the media have had the kits for a couple of days, follow-up with phone calls to editors or reporters to arrange the interviews.

Many people find this hard to do, and it is hard if you don't know how. Fortunately, learning how is not that difficult.

Just follow this procedure: Identify yourself and explain briefly why you're calling. If the person received your Media Information Kit, ask if he or she would like an interview. If not, don't argue. Simply say something like: "If you change your mind, or if you have any questions about the material, please give me a call." And then hang up.

If the editor or reporter says your material never arrived – which may, in fact, be a cover-up for the fact that it was thrown out – offer to send another package by courier right away. Then you close the conversation with something like: "If you decide you want an interview or have any questions about the material, please give me a call."

If you feel the itch to give a hard sell, remember this: One of the many axes that Kenneth Kidd said he and his colleagues have to grind concerns "publicists who become argumentative if you tell them you're not interested in their story, which, they maintain, has revolutionary consequences for all of mankind." Kidd added caustically, but truthfully, "Irritating journalists, making them feel defensive at the very name of some PR agencies, is not something for which clients should have to pay."

The key to success in arranging interviews is to come up with the right peg in the first place. Give the journalist a reason for interviewing you. Asking the local talk show host to interview your new chairman on the air may get you a lukewarm response. But quote the chairman as saying that another Hydro rate increase will cost thousands of jobs or that you've developed a new type of mortgage that will make housing more affordable for the average person, and you've practically guaranteed yourself some air time.

Preparing for Interviews

Now that you've got your interview set up, how do you prepare for it?

The first thing to do is identify the one, two or, at most, three key points that you want to make in the interview. These key points are the reason you went to all the trouble to get the interview in the first place, so they'd better be the points you end up making. That's what managing the media is all about.

To help you maintain control over the interview, prepare a "crib sheet" containing the questions you anticipate the reporter will ask and the answers you would like to give. The crib sheet is a kind of script. Its purpose is to make each question you might be asked work to your advantage. You do this by using each question as an opportunity to make at least one of your main points.

For example, one of your main points might be to show that your company contributes to the wealth of Canada through extensive exports. You expect that the interviewer will ask about the North American Free Trade Agreement, interprovincial barriers to trade, reforms of the corporate tax structure, labour-management relations and a host of other major public policy issues.

To each of these questions, you can give a relevant, brief and straightforward answer, then turn the question around to your purposes with a remark like:

"The one thing the unions must understand when making wage demands is that we must remain competitive on international markets. Our company added $150 million to the wealth of Canada and supported 500 jobs through exports. It would be a shame if these benefits were jeopardized by unreasonable union demands."

Try to make time to rehearse the interview. Arrange a "bear pit" session, in which several members of your company or association can assault the interviewee with as many nasty questions as you can think of. Use the crib sheet as a guide in the bear pit session, and use the session to revise the sheet.

Giving Media Interviews

The most important thing to remember about speaking to the media is that nothing, I repeat, nothing is "off the record." Everything you say can be used by the reporter.

When I was a correspondent for Reuters in Denmark, there were daily "off the record" briefings with then-British Prime Minister Douglas-Home when he came to Copenhagen to attend a meeting of NATO members. "Off the record" in those situations had a very specific meaning. We could report what was said, but not who said it. In fact, the Prime Minister, himself, would often tell us how we could attribute certain statements; for example, to "a British diplomatic source" or "an informed NATO source." This arrangement was developed by the Prime Minister to serve his own ends – he could use the media to float trial balloons. If they fell flat, he could dissociate himself completely. If they proved successful, he could take credit.

Now, we didn't have to respect the Prime Minister's wishes. We could have quoted him directly. But that would have been the last time the offending journalist would have been invited to a briefing. "Off the record," then, means nothing more than a reporter's word that he'll respect you as a source. The question you should ask yourself is, how well can you trust the reporter? And how much clout do you have with him?

My advice is to play it safe: Don't tell a reporter anything you don't want to see in print. The interview begins with the first words of greeting, so stick as closely to your agenda as possible.

For telephone interviews, keep the crib sheet in front of you for constant reference, but do not sound as though you are reading from a prepared text. This will come with practice, although it helps if the answers on the crib sheet are written in a colloquial style.

You don't want the reporter to know that you've got a crib sheet and you most emphatically do not want the reporter to see it. Let the reporter think of the nasty questions on his own – don't lend a helping hand. So you're more restricted in live interviews, since you can't be seen reading from the crib sheet. You can refer to it, if it is held discreetly in your view only – say in a binder – but do not use it during interviews that are being photographed, filmed or videotaped.

If you don't know the answer to a question, say so. But keep in mind that you still may be able to use the question to make one of your primary points.

Remember how to say "no." Not every question must be answered. If a reporter requests confidential information, say so, directly but politely, and if possible, use the question as an opportunity to make one of your key points. "I'm sorry I can't disclose the unit production costs of our Class A widgets, since that information is confidential, but I can say that the combination of advanced technology and a highly productive workforce enables us to produce a product of unbeatable quality at a competitive price."

And finally, don't be embarrassed into saying something you might regret merely to fill up a real or imagined void in the interview. It's the reporter's job to ask the questions. When you've answered them to your satisfaction, stop speaking. A reporter may often purposely create a hiatus to goad you into saying more than you really intended. If this happens, even during a live radio or TV interview, just sit calmly and patiently, with a pleasant expression on your face. Any subsequent silence will embarrass the reporter, not you. And in a few seconds, the reporter will be flustered for something to say, not you.

Giving the Interview to a Print Reporter

Preparing the content of an interview should be pretty much the same for print, radio or television interviews. You get your message down pat and figure out how to express it briefly in response to any type of question. But there are significant differences in how your message should be delivered to print, radio and TV reporters.

The print reporter may wish to record the interview, but the audio tape is usually used only as backup. The primary source material for the eventual article will generally come from the reporter's written notes. If it's not in the notes, it might never see the light of print. So, when you give print interviews, help the reporter get your message fully and accurately by slowing down or pausing when you see the reporter hurriedly scribbling notes on the pad.

Most conscientious reporters will come to the interview with questions already written down. You'll find that throughout the interview, the reporter will take time to leaf through his or her pad to check whether this or that question has been asked or answered. The resulting silence can be deafening and unnerving. Don't worry. Just sit calmly and quietly while the reporter does his or her thing. Don't feel compelled to fill that void of silence with meaningless, and thus potentially harmful, chatter.

You should also resist a similar urge that may strike you at the end of answers, when you've stopped talking, but the reporter has not yet stopped jotting down your remarks. Learn to live with that silence, too. The relatively leisurely pace and informality of print interviews gives you welcomed latitude. You can pause briefly during an answer to look up a pertinent fact or two. And you can break a tense moment by offering the reporter another cup of coffee or by temporarily diverting the conversation to an innocuous topic.

Print interviews bring you close to the reporter, but keep you distant from the reader. What's going to be paraded before the public is neither your direct image nor your actual voice. Aside from any still photographs that may accompany the article, the story will be a verbal portrait painted by the reporter, largely on the basis of the reporter's first-hand impressions gathered during the interview.

You should, therefore, use the interview to demonstrate the salient aspects of your personality. You can be witty or dry, jovial or sombre, introspective or extroverted. You'll have anywhere from 15 minutes to an hour or more to show yourself in various poses. These poses, however, should be real. You should not try to create a false image – to appear to be something that you're not, no matter how appealing that image may be to you. Your principal objective in developing a rapport with the reporter is to establish your knowledge, wisdom and credibility. Your goal is to ensure that the reporter believes and respects what you say during the interview. Only then will your remarks be reported accurately, comprehensively and credibly.

What makes this process so different from broadcast interviews is that you are in dialogue with the print reporter. Your actions and responses and the reporter's actions and responses galvanize into perceptions by the reporter of who and what you are – and how the reporter interprets those perceptions will dictate how you are portrayed in the newspaper or magazine article.

Giving the Interview to Broadcast Media

Things get sort of reversed when you are interviewed by a radio or television reporter. The interviews are more formal, in part because you must remain physically immobile. You can't wander about the room or even sway back and forth in your chair when you're before the camera or microphone. But more significantly, with radio or television, you're playing not to a single person – the reporter – with whom you develop an active dialogue. You're playing directly to the thousands of listeners and viewers. And with them, instead of engaging in a dialogue, you're giving a monologue. The radio or TV reporter doesn't intervene as much as the print reporter between you and the public. The print reporter may say that you hesitated when giving the answer, that you appeared either nervous or self-assured, that you smiled sarcastically or frowned with genuine concern. But the television viewers will see these things for themselves.

At the same time, you are not in direct conversation with the audience. Unlike the print reporter with whom you can establish rapport during an interview, the radio or TV audience does not formulate the question, ask it, evaluate your verbal or nonverbal reaction and then form an impression or make a judgement and ask a follow-up question, thus giving you the opportunity to expand on your answers or clarify a point.

When it comes to radio and TV, you're on a one-way street; the audience merely eavesdrops on an edited portion of a conversation you had with the reporter, evaluates your responses, but gives no feedback. You've got to establish a positive rapport with the mass radio and TV audience in every answer you give during the interview, and no answer should be longer than 15 or 20 seconds, since that is likely the longest that any single broadcast portion of the interview will be. So the content and style of each answer you give assume paramount importance.

Of course, the radio or television reporter can slant a story every bit as well as the print reporter. After all, the reporter can try to set the tone of the interview not only by the questions that he or she asks but also in how they are asked. And the reporter will write and tape an introductory and closing narrative (which will or will not be used, at the discretion of the producer or news editor). So developing a constructive rapport with the broadcast reporter is as important as developing a good rapport with the print reporter. It's just that you don't have as much scope and opportunity in a broadcast interview situation. With the print journalist, you've got virtually the entire interview. With the broadcast journalist, you've got just a few minutes before and after the taping to discuss the parameters of the interview, to provide any detailed background information and to generate any needed goodwill.

And, of course, you can, and should, use those five or 10 minutes of chatter with the reporter before and after a radio or TV interview to establish your character and credibility, and hope that a favourable impression will predispose the reporter to your side of the story being told. But the inescapable fact remains: if you come across as shifty, evasive, ill-informed or mendacious in the brief broadcast portion of the interview, anything that the reporter or newscaster says about you in the narrative portion will count for naught.

Ten Tips on TV Demeanour, Dress and Style

The impression you make on a reporter may colour the story that eventually emerges. How you act, the tone of your voice, the clothing you wear and the setting of the interview are, therefore, important in every interview situation. But these take on added importance in television interviews, where you are creating an impression not just with the reporter, but with the thousands, perhaps millions, of people who will see you when the story is aired.

Special care must be taken, not only in what you say and how you say it, but also in how you look and act. To ensure that your appearance before the camera will project a positive image and enhance your credibility, adhere to the following 10 tips.

1. Your demeanour should be open, comfortable and relaxed, with the degree of seriousness appropriate to the topic. Your facial expressions and your body language will speak louder than your words. Sit stiffly, and you'll erect a barrier that will block communication between you and your audience. Fidget, and you'll appear nervous and evasive. Look jovial when discussing misfortune, and you'll appear to be cruel and insensitive. Remain tight-lipped and stern in the face of humour, and you'll look like an unfriendly stuffed shirt.

But show interest in the interviewer, and you'll appear to be sincere. Treat the interviewer with respect, and you will earn the respect of your audience. Give your eyes, eyebrows and mouth freedom – to show concern when concern is warranted, surprise when surprise is warranted, contemplation when contemplation is warranted – and your audience will regard you as honest, thoughtful and sympathetic.

And finally, if you don't know the most appropriate emotion to show in response to a particular interview or question, cultivate a neutral, but pleasing, facial expression. Ingrid Bergman was once asked how she managed to portray such an intense range of feelings that always seemed appropriate to the situations confronting her characters. She said she sometimes did not fully understand the situation or know exactly how she should act in it, in which case she said she would merely look blank – in essence, showing no emotion – and the people watching the film would ascribe to her character what they, themselves, were feeling. Each person watching your interview on television will attribute to you the feelings or attitude that he or she, individually, believes you ought to have.

2. What you wear reflects on what your are. Your clothing, like your demeanour, can heighten or diminish your credibility. Neatness and cleanliness are essential. It is difficult to regard someone who wears wrinkled trousers or skirts, has ring around the collar and frayed lapels as authoritative, knowledgeable and truthful – with the possible exception of certain academic stereotypes whose reputation

for knowledge and honesty is too often offset by an image of imprac-
ticality and absent-mindedness.

Avoid flashy colours and strong, complex patterns. Not only
does this type of clothing convey an image of the unscrupulous used-
car salesman, it can be highly distracting on the TV screen.

You see a lot of executives being interviewed in shirt-sleeves. The
idea is to make the person appear to be a friendly, hard-working person of the people. And it may work, in some cases. But I would not
recommend it. It is difficult to look well groomed in shirt sleeves, and
the image on television of someone in shirt-sleeves is less appealing
and less defined than someone wearing a gray or blue business jacket.

It will not work if you don't feel comfortable without a jacket
on. If you're going to feel self-conscious in your shirt-sleeves, then
for heaven's sake wear a jacket. Whatever the assumed benefits of the
cultivated informal look might be, they will be more than offset by
your involuntary display of discomfort.

Second, your attire should reflect the role in which the interview
is casting you. Each persona has its own uniform. Lawyers, doctors,
accountants, writers, graphic artists – all have identifiable styles of
clothing. So, if you're a doctor, wearing a white examination coat is
not only appropriate, but effective. Likewise, a designer can get away
with wearing a sweater and open shirt, while such informality might
tend to diminish the stature, and thus the credibility, of the Chairman
of the Board.

But a lot may depend on circumstances, which brings us to the
third point – that your style of dress should be appropriate to the
nature of the interview and where it's taking place. It may prove
advantageous, for example, to be in your shirt-sleeves when answering media questions in your office or plant about your organization's
plans to cut costs and improve productivity. This is the time to
emphasize your willingness, both literally and figuratively, to roll up
your sleeves and get down to some really hard work. But such informality would not be appropriate, say, at a media scrum or full-scale
news conference at your annual meeting. A business suit is the proper
attire for both men and women at such a function, and therefore
becomes the proper attire for interviews given at that function.

3. Look at the interviewer, not the camera. In most interview situations, the television audience is a third party, a kind of eavesdropper
on a conversation between two other people, in much the same way

that the theatregoer is listening in on the action taking place on stage. As the interviewee, your credibility derives from your interaction with the interviewer.

The exception to this rule is the long-distance interview of the kind seen on "Prime Time News" and US network news, where the person asking the questions is sitting in a studio and the person answering them may be miles away in another city, appearing only on a studio monitor. In this situation – called a double-ender – the interviewer and the television viewer have the same perspective of the interviewee. So in order to appear to be looking at the interviewer, you look into the camera. You do not, however, want to stare into the camera and end up looking like a fixated robot lacking true judgement or intelligence. To give your appearance some vitality and interest, periodically change the position of your head slightly and make minimal shifts in the point at which your eyes are focusing. By minimal I mean something as small as from one rim of the camera lens to the other.

4.   Don't squint. Studio lights and the reflectors brought into your office for television interviews can be harsh. Get used to them and don't show your discomfort. Rapidly blinking your eyes or squinting to lessen the sting of the lights will only reflect badly on you, making you look squeamish and evasive.

5.   Minimize your movements. Because your face and torso will fill up most of the TV screen, any movement you make will be greatly exaggerated. Most of us punctuate our speech with numerous conscious or unconscious movements. We rock back and forth in our chair, sway from side to side, turn our head or let our eyes wander across the room, and if we're standing, jingle the change in our trouser pocket. Your hands can be especially troublesome. Keep them away from your face. Hands flying across the screen are an annoying distraction, and certain hand movements, such as covering your mouth, rubbing your nose or pulling your ear, will cast doubt upon your trustworthiness and erode your credibility. Become aware of any of these mannerisms you may have, then keep them under control during television interviews.

The next challenge is to do this without appearing to be tense and stiff. Let your body relax; loosen the muscles in your arms, shoulders and face. And then raise an eyebrow, furrow your brow, crack a smile or cock your head to emphasize a point. The idea is not to be utterly immobile; it is to be economical in your movements.

6.   If you're seated at a desk, lean slightly forward with your back straight, your forearms resting on the table and your hands clasped. This will make you appear to be outgoing, communicative and confident without being arrogant. This pose will also prevent you rocking, swaying or gesticulating.

7.   If you're sitting in a stool or chair with no desk or table in front of you, cross your legs, with clasped hands resting on your lap. Crossing your legs accomplishes two purposes. First, it's a modest pose – sitting with your legs spread is inappropriate, for both men and women. Second, crossing your legs forces you to sit up, and it gives your body a sharper, more angular and, thus, more interesting appearance.

8.   If you're standing, relax, but don't slouch or hunch your shoulders. You'll probably catch the best pose by keeping your feet about six inches apart with one foot slightly ahead of the other. What to do with your arms and hands can be a problem. You don't want them dangling limply at your side, yet you don't want to flail them about, either. Moving your arms and hands too much will make you look aggressive and irrational.

Your best bet may be to put one hand in your trouser or skirt pocket, with the other arm held at your side or slightly bent at the elbow. Then you can occasionally rotate the wrist of your free arm or flick the fingers of that hand to emphasize a point. These minimal movements will project confidence, but not aggressiveness or arrogance. If you place a hand in your pocket, keep it still. Don't create an annoying diversion by rattling your change. Alternatively, you may hold both arms in front of your body, with one hand held over the other.

9.   Don't clutter your desk with papers in an attempt to look busy. You'll only succeed in looking disorganized. And be sure to hide any sensitive or confidential papers. The eye of the camera sees all.

10. Ensure that the setting projects the appropriate image of your organization. If you're giving an interview on your organization's cost-management program, don't steer the reporter and camera crew to your fancy, mahogany-paneled boardroom. A modest office or conference room would be appropriate. You may, for example, want

to conduct an interview at your company's factory, if it's sufficiently attractive and modern to project your company as a technologically advanced industry leader. But if black smoke is spewing out of the stack, or the area is piled with refuse waiting to be carted away or you are involved in a delicate situation with the workforce that may prompt some employees to use the interview with you as an opportunity to grab some media attention, avoid the pitfalls, and hold the interview somewhere else.

IN BRIEF

Arranging Media Interviews

1. Establish a news peg.
2. Write a news release based on your news peg.
3. Assemble a Media Information Kit.
4. Anticipate how many interviews you might have, and set aside sufficient time for them.
5. Distribute Media Information Kits to your selected media list, timing them to arrive about a week before you want the interviews.
6. Follow up with phone calls to editors and reporters to arrange interviews.

Preparing for Media Interviews

1. Identify two or three key organizational goals you intend to advance through the interview.
2. Identify as best you can the topics that the interviewer intends to cover.
3. Identify the one, two, or three aspects of each topic that will best help you achieve your objectives.
4. On the basis of Steps 1, 2 and 3, prepare a crib sheet containing the questions you anticipate you'll be asked and the way they should be answered.
5. Rehearse the interview in "bear pit" sessions, revising the crib sheet, as required.

Giving the Interview

1. Nothing is "off the record." Everything you say can be published or broadcast.
2. Remember the main points that you want to make, and reiterate them whenever possible; conversely, avoid belabouring irrelevant points.
3. Be familiar with the crib sheet, and refer to it during telephone interviews. But never sound as though you are reading from a text.
4. If you don't know the answer to a question say so – and get back to the reporter later with the answer.
5. If the reporter requests confidential information that you do not want to give, say so – directly, but politely.
6. When you've said your piece, stop talking, and wait for the next question.

Added Tips for TV Interviews

1. Your demeanour should be open, comfortable and relaxed, with the degree of seriousness appropriate to the topic.
2. Dress appropriately and neatly.
   - Avoid flashy colours and strong, complex patterns.
   - Clothing should be clean and unwrinkled.
   - If the interview is in your office, wear your jacket – do not appear in your shirtsleeves.
   - If the interview is outside your office, wear the clothing appropriate to the surroundings.
3. Look at the interviewer, not the camera.
4. Don't squint from possibly harsh TV lights – it'll make you look evasive.
5. Minimize movements – your face and torso will fill up most of the TV screen and any body movements will appear greatly exaggerated.
6. If you're seated at a desk, lean slightly forward with your back straight, your forearms resting on the table and your hands clasped.

7. If you're sitting in a stool or chair with no desk or table in front of you, cross your legs, with clasped hands resting on your lap.

8. If you're standing, relax, but don't slouch, keeping your feet about six inches apart, with one foot slightly ahead of the other. You may put one hand in your trouser pocket or hanging at your side with the other arm hanging at your side or slightly bent at the elbow.

9. Hide any sensitive or confidential papers – the eye of the camera sees all.

10. Ensure that the setting projects the appropriate image of your organization.

The Tools
For Telling Your
Story Effectively

One of the most difficult things to judge is newsworthiness. How do you know when a story is news or not?

You've probably been told a million times that a story is newsworthy when the editor says it is. That's true, as far as it goes. If the editor believes a story to be news, it gets printed or broadcast; if not, it doesn't.

But does that help you, the media relations person, decide whether a story you want to tell is newsworthy? Probably not, unless you can have some insight into the editor's thought processes.

What Makes a Story Newsworthy?

Most editors go through a check list – sometimes consciously, sometimes unconsciously – when deciding whether to pursue a story.

Here's the checklist that I use.

1. *Relevance* Will the story have an impact on the daily lives of the people who read the newspaper, listen to the radio or watch television?

I want to go to the Grey Cup game. Where can I get tickets and how much do they cost? The government is going to raise taxes. How much will I have to pay and what tax loopholes can I find?

If your company dominates a community – like Inco in Sudbury – just about anything your company does is news. But in Toronto, Inco vies with thousands of other corporate enterprises for coverage of its activities, and what's newsworthy in Sudbury might get spiked in Toronto.

2. *Topicality* Does the story deal with a major issue of the day or lasting passion of the people? Your comments about the new budget may be newsworthy on budget night or the day after, but they're not

news the following week. A few years ago, the Canadian Baseball Hall of Fame unveiled a portrait of Babe Ruth to commemorate a home run he hit at Hanlan's Point, the first and only homer the Babe hit in the minor leagues. The news conference, held at the height of the pennant race in September, attracted a slew of reporters and got decent coverage. I doubt any media would have bothered to attend if the portrait were unveiled during Grey Cup week or at the beginning of the Stanley Cup playoffs.

3.   *Human interest*   Does the story touch on an emotion or experience shared by most people? What made Shakespeare so popular through the ages was, in part, his ability to express the human condition – "Parting is such sweet sorrow," "Et tu, Brute." We've all felt the joy of being in love and the sadness at a temporary parting, and we all know what it's like to be stabbed in the back. We are all essentially voyeurs, and a story that gives us a glimpse into the shared secrets of existence – into the emotions of the people involved – is news.

4.   *Entertainment value*   Anything that stimulates our curiosity, fires our fancy, excites our passion or hits our jocular vein is news. This is the world of man-bites-dog, flagpole sitting, discovery of the missing link, the Loch Ness monster, the exploits of the rich and famous and the foibles of the pretentious and the inept. Entertainment value is really the funny side of human interest.

5.   *Controversy*   The world loves a good mud fight, and the more controversial a subject, the greater the public drive to soak up the details and the greater the media's desire to provide them. The only trouble with controversy: As one of the players, you may provide news, but the chances are you won't look good. The media – and through them, the general public – will have a good time at your expense. So avoid being dragged into controversy. This doesn't mean that you should never publicly express your views on controversial subjects. What it does mean is that you should avoid gratuitous attacks on other people or other organizations. Put another way: When discussing contentious situations, talk about the issues, not the personalities.

Relevance, topicality, human interest, entertainment value and controversy. This is how I define newsworthiness for myself. Other media relations people and journalists may use other words and have other lists to describe what is and what is not news. The fact is, news-worthiness is a highly imprecise concept that is as subjective as it is universal. It is as variable as each individual and as unchanging as our shared humanity.

So if it turns you on, it's probably news.

A few years back, Denison opened a new plant to produce yttri-um – which is used in televisions, fluorescent lights, lasers and other high-tech equipment – as a byproduct of its uranium operations. The local media gave the official opening extensive coverage, pegging their stories on the jobs that the plant would create.

This wouldn't fly in Toronto, Vancouver or Montreal, other than as maybe a paragraph in the business section of the daily newspapers or a write-up in such trade publications as the *Northern Miner*.

To get broader coverage, you need a good news peg. You've got to find something about the plant that makes it appealing to the general public, that makes it newsworthy, that gives it relevance, topicali-ty, human interest or entertainment value.

And, of course, the decision on whether to seek broader cover-age would depend on whether telling your story to the public in a particular way will help you achieve your organizational goals.

How to Tell Your Story

So let's say you've identified a newsworthy story about your organi-zation. How do you tell it?

As a reporter for the *Toronto Star* back in the '70s, I spent three days researching Connaught Laboratories. I was given the assignment following Connaught's announcement that it didn't have a vaccine on hand to combat Swine Flu. The lab had come under heavy criticism, and I was told to "find out what was wrong at Connaught."

It was an enlightening experience, especially since the much-besieged lab was, in fact, conducting very interesting and potentially valuable research into developing an artificial pancreas and a new form of polio vaccine.

The story I handed in to the city editor dutifully recorded those activities, painting a picture of a modern and well-run research facili-ty that was still saddled by earlier business misjudgements. But not a word of the innovative research appeared in print. It was all edited out, leaving the impression that Connaught was deficient in research, a perception that was even captured in the headline.

My first inclination was to blame the editors for being so damned stupid. But looking back, I think that I might have written the story more effectively so that what I regarded as its most salient features would not have been deleted.

Connaught was also disappointed in the story. They had opened their labs to me. They had spent many hours explaining their operations and had exposed themselves to public scrutiny during a controversial time in their history in hopes of setting the record straight and getting much-needed recognition for some of their innovative research programs.

They had some justification for blaming me for writing an inferior story. But if they had done their job of relating with me – the media – just a bit more thoroughly, they might have helped me get a better grip on what is, after all, a highly technical operation. In the end, instead of lamenting negative media coverage, they might have congratulated themselves on engineering an effective public relations coup.

If they had better understood the constraints I was under, they might have organized the material they gave me in a more comprehensible fashion. For example, I was given no written material describing in lay language the various research projects the lab was undertaking. There was no written history of the company. I had no organization chart, no biographical sketches of key executives or researchers.

Brochures, annual reports, fact sheets, internal and external publications and news releases are tremendous editorial aids. They heighten a reporter's understanding, ensure greater accuracy and focus attention where you want it to be focused. Of these materials, only one – the news release – is regarded strictly as a media relations tool. The others are normally the preserve of other functions – the annual report of investor relations, brochures of numerous other departments such as marketing and human resources, and fact sheets of any of a number of technical areas.

But these tools also play a vital role in effective media relations, and producing them requires close cooperation and coordination among many departments. The communications tools of virtually all departments can, and should, be written and designed with possible media exploitation in mind.

An organization that spends tens of thousands of dollars to write, design and print an annual report, but does not structure the document so it can be used as a tool to sell the organization – to customers, clients, employees, prospective employees, the power brokers in the public and private sectors, the media and other important publics – is wasting most of its money.

Conversely, an organization that relegates public or media relations to one of the lower rungs on the ladder of budget priorities, could be engaging in a costly exercise of false economy. What good is a John Olerud, if he steps up to the plate without a bat?

The Media Information Kit

So here you are, standing in the media relations batter's box. What kind of bat should you swing? What tools do you use? The basic package is the Media Information Kit, and a complete one should contain:

- A news release – the basic form of virtually all media communications.
- Full texts of speeches or other relevant company statements.
- A general-purpose corporate brochure.
- Printed pamphlets, with photographs if possible, dealing with your new product, technology or factory.
- "Fact sheets" giving relevant background to the issue or development you're publicizing.
- Biographical sketches and glossy 5x7 or 8x10 photographs of key people.
- Covering letter for editors and reporters.

Not every Media Information Kit is the same, however. Which of the materials you use in any given situation would depend on three key factors:

1. The nature of your media program. Generally speaking, the more important the announcement, the more you will include in your kit. Announcing unspectacular quarterly earnings may require nothing more than a news release and a copy of your interim report. But if your company is launching a major program to diversify and expand its operations, you should provide a full Media Information Kit that would explain the ramifications of what you're doing and why that's important to your company and its shareholders.

2. The frequency of your announcements. If you're regularly feeding the media with news releases about your activities, you shouldn't include copies of your annual report, brochures or bio-graphical sketches of your top executives in every announcement. You'd be wasting your money and alienating the editors and reporters you were trying to reach. Avoid excessive duplication.

3.   **The way you are distributing the information to the media.** You can use a full kit if you are delivering it by hand, by courier or by mail. But if you're using electronic distribution, you're limited to your news release, a note to editors and a brief backgrounder.

As a rule of thumb, it should take no longer than about 30 minutes for a reporter to read and digest the salient information contained in the Media Information Kit. You may, on occasion, break this rule by including lengthy documents (such as annual reports, detailed prod-uct brochures or the full texts of complex reports) that the reporter may use either as background material to be filed away for future use or as information to be incorporated in the story at hand. In either event, if there are specific statements, recommendations or facts con-tained in these documents that you want reported, then highlight them in an accompanying fact sheet or executive summary.

Back in the late 1980s, Amoco Canada and Dome Petroleum held a news conference to announce details of their proposed merger. More than a hundred media people descended on the Royal York Hotel in Toronto for the news conference. The president of each company was there to answer media questions. And the PR depart-ments of each company worked feverously to prepare a comprehen-sive Media Information Kit, replete with news releases (there were two, which in my view is one too many), fact sheets on the two com-panies and the full text of the merger contract. The only deficiency of the package – aside from the overabundance of news releases – was the absence of a summary containing the salient points of the merger contract.

It is unreasonable to expect a reporter, writing on deadline, to have the time to read, analyze and understand a 55-page, single-spaced document written in a language (legalese) that is often incom-prehensible to the lay person. Omitting the summary increases the likelihood that reporters may ignore or distort some of the key provi-sions of the merger contract.

I don't want to come down too hard on the PR people who assembled the kit. They were under tremendous pressure and said they simply didn't have the time to prepare the summary. I wonder, however, whether that was the real problem. How long would it have taken the lawyers or company executives who wrote or negotiated the contract to prepare a list of its dozen or so most significant elements? I suspect this didn't happen because of poor communications between the public relations people and the companies' senior executives. The accountants can't do their job if the production people don't show anyone their bills and the marketing people don't disclose their revenue. By the same token, public relations practitioners can't do their job if senior management doesn't take the time to provide them with vital information and to answer questions.

The News Release As Good Journalism

When you tell your story to the media, tell it right. And if you send out a news release, follow the principles and style of good journalism, because if you don't, two things could happen:

The media will ignore your release, and to the editor or reporter whose desk it crossed, you'll appear as if you don't know what you're doing, or don't care. The next time you send a release, it may get spiked without even being read.

Or the reporter will try to decipher your release, and in this translation process, get some key points all wrong.

In either case, you'll come out the loser. Remember, you've got to build your image with the media. And you do that by giving the media what it wants, which is a good story presented in a usable way.

Not long after I took my first corporate PR job, one of the executives handed me a news release and said, "Get this to the media, willya, Ed?" I looked over the page and I didn't understand a word of it. It was one long sentence of convoluted jargon.

"This is unreadable and unusable. I can't send that to the media."

"Oh, that doesn't matter," I was told. "We don't care if the media use it. We're only sending it to meet the disclosure requirements of the Ontario Securities Commission."

"No," I answered, "If it goes to the media, it goes in usable form. If it's gobbledygook, it'll get spiked. And the next time we send a release, that'll probably get spiked too, without ever being read. We'd lose control of the media."

I finally got my point across and we started to prepare the release from scratch, with me playing reporter. I probed, in order to understand what the release was all about. What does this phrase mean? What would happen if? Why is it important to a potential investor?

As he answered my questions, I wrote the release as I would a news story – something that would be easy to read and would make sense to the wide range of people who would pick up tomorrow's paper.

In the end, we came up with something. It was only a few paragraphs long, dealing with an equity issue the company was announcing. The next day, the *Globe and Mail* published the story word for word as it appeared in the release. And the publicity made it that much easier to sell the new stock issue.

How to Format a News Release

All news releases should follow the correct format, which means that they must contain certain essential elements.

Release Time   The first thing you'll need is a release time. If there is no restriction on when your news can be used, write "For Immediate Release" at the top of the page. If you don't want the release to be used before a certain time, say so. If it's reporting a speech that won't be given until one o'clock the following day, write "Not For Use Before 1 pm EDT, Friday, October 29, 1993" or "Embargoed Until 1 pm EDT, Friday, October 29, 1993."

Use embargoes sparingly. You have no way of ensuring that they will be kept, and once one newspaper or radio or TV station breaks your embargo, everyone else will follow suit. The policy of the Canadian Press, for example, is to honour all embargoes until someone else doesn't.

For this reason, you should never make an early release of sensitive information – such as your earnings statement, layoffs or a plant shutdown, the launch of new products – in hopes that the media will keep your news confidential until the intended release time.

Headline   When I first began giving media relations seminars in the fall of 1985, I argued against putting headlines in news releases. I read somewhere that they take up valuable space that the newspaper itself would want to use for its own headline.

That reasoning is outmoded. Virtually all news releases, if they are going to be used, are given to a reporter to work on. The news story that emerges is then entered into a computer terminal. Any subsequent changes to the story, and that includes putting on the headline, are made directly on the computer or from a computer printout, not on your news release.

The headline on your release does, however, serve a vital function: It quickly tells the editor what the release is all about. And that makes it easier to sell your story.

Dateline   The third element of the news release format is the dateline. You begin the text of all news releases with the name of the city where the news is taking place or from which the announcement you're making originates. This is followed by the date the news is to be released. An acceptable variation is to place the date at the top of the page and include only the name of the city in the dateline.

"More"   The fourth formatting rule is to end all but the last page with the word "more" centred below the last line of text, and never end a page in the middle of a paragraph. On the last page, just below the final paragraph of the release, centre the number "30." This means "the end" in journalese, and probably originated in the days when news dispatches were sent by telegraph using Morse code. To avoid confusion, the letter X was used instead of a period at the end of a sentence; two Xs meant the end of a paragraph and three Xs indicated the end of a story. At some point, someone made the connection between "XXX" and the Roman numeral for the number 30 and chose to use the shorter form.

Contact   The final element of the release format is the name and phone number of the media contact. In most cases that would be a media or public relations person. At the very end of the release, give the name, title and office and after-hours telephone number of the contact person.
It is preferable to have just one contact person – who ought to be someone well trained in the art of giving interviews. The more contacts you list, the greater the chance that you will lose control of the story, which usually happens when reporters play one spokesperson against the other. For this reason, I do not recommend listing the organization's media relations person along with one or more experts on the topic of the release. All media calls should go to the media relations person, who would then determine whether to handle the interview or to bring in the expert.

CATHEDRAL OF THE TRANSFIGURATION

Information Office: P.O. Box 524, Gormley, Ontario, L0H 1G0 (416) 887-5706

<u>**FOR IMMEDIATE RELEASE**</u>

World's largest peal of bells arrives at Markham cathedral

MARKHAM, Ontario, July 7, 1986 -- The world's largest peal of bells arrived at their new home today, the Slovak Cathedral of the Transfiguration, following a 28-day, 4,000-mile land and sea journey from a foundry in France.

The three bells -- weighing 37,000 pounds, 21,000 pounds and 13,000 pounds -- were lifted by crane from the truck that drove them from the port of Halifax and hoisted into their permanent home in the 210-foot-high centre tower of the as-yet unfinished cathedral.

The cathedral and its cornerstone were blessed by Pope John Paul II during his visit to Canada in September 1984. This marked the first time that a Roman Pontiff consecrated a church in North America.

Cardinal Carter, Archbishop of Toronto, will bless the bells, and they will be rung for the first time, at a public ceremony on Sunday, August 10, 1986. They will be christened St. Stephen, St. Anne and the Prophet Daniel. A carving on each bell depicts a scene from the life of its namesake. St. Stephen, the largest of the three and the 13th largest single bell in the world, is dedicated to Pope John Paul.

(more)

Eparchy of Sts. Cyril and Methodius of Slovaks of the Byzantine Rite in Canada

If you have operations in different parts of the country and if the local media in those sites would be interested in the story, then it would be advisable to list contacts in those locations – provided that these individuals were properly trained.

Make sure, though, that the contact or contacts can be reached at the phone number you've listed. Nothing is more irritating for a reporter on deadline than to call the contact, only to be informed that he or she is on holiday in the Bahamas for the next two weeks.

Some people prefer to put the contact name at the top of the release, and there is nothing wrong with this.

How to Write a News Release

The most important thing to remember about writing a news release is that you are producing a news story. So write it the way a good reporter would.

1. Whenever possible use the active voice. Make it: "Everyone had a good time," not "A good time was had by all." As the nomenclature suggests, the active voice projects movement and energy, and that makes your story more enjoyable to read.

2. Use the present tense when you want to increase the "shelf life" of the story and the action described is not fixed to a particular time. This is useful in featurish news releases that will not be overtaken by events and is especially important in releases that are distributed by mail, and thus will arrive on an editor's desk several days after it was cleared for publication. Magazines, weekly newspapers, radio or television magazine shows or, in some cases, even daily newspapers may be more likely to use such a release if it does not appear to be time sensitive. Using the present tense ("he says," instead of "he said") will frequently accomplish this.

But do not use the present tense in a release dealing with a breaking story. If an announcement was made at a particular time or if the release focuses on an action that took place at a particular time, then stick to the past tense both as a means of fixing the story at the appropriate moment and as a means of conveying that sense of timeliness to the media. Such items as your company's earnings and a plant shutdown, strike, accident or other crisis are breaking stories and should therefore be written in the past tense – "The ABC Company today announced net earning for 1993 of $3.5 million, up from $2.3 million in 1992."

3.   **Avoid jargon.**   It doesn't impress editors. It turns them off and the release won't be used. Your message will be changed by the editor or reporter, and in being changed it may be distorted. You lose control over your message.

When I was working as an editor at the *New York Times*, I served as chairman of the Newspaper Guild's Job Evaluation Committee, which wrote job descriptions and negotiated pay scales for new and existing positions. This has nothing to do directly with news releases, but it makes a point. I was trying to get a newsroom job upgraded, and I made my case to the industrial relations manager, figuring it would be the first of many negotiating sessions. But I was in for a pleasant surprise. Within a week, the industrial relations manager got back to me with the good news – I got the upgrading.

"How come?" I asked.

"Because," the industrial relations manager replied, "when you described the job to me, you made sense. I understood what you were talking about. But when I went to the department manager to get his side of the story, all I got was a bunch of journalistic jargon. He was using terms I didn't understand. So I figured if you made sense and he didn't, then you must be right."

The moral of that story is: Try to impress someone by using big words or incomprehensible jargon, and you'll just end up showing yourself the door.

4.   **Write a strong lead.**   The important thing about writing news releases is to organize your thoughts. List all the points you want to make, prioritize them, and choose one for your lead paragraph. The point that you use in your lead should meet two criteria:
- It must be near the top of your priority list.
- It must be newsworthy.

The lead is the most important paragraph in your release. It's the grabber that will get the editor to read further. So take the time to write a good one. Both as a reporter and as a public relations practitioner, my best news stories or news releases were those on which I spent most of my time on the lead paragraph. If your lead is good, the rest of the story will follow with relative ease.

The lead should include as many of the five Ws as possible – the Who, What, When, Where and Why. But don't torture the lead to get them all in. You do have a second paragraph, or a third, if necessary, to get all the relevant information in. So you should also prioritize the five Ws. If the person making the announcement is news, then begin with the name of the person. If the news is that a new product is on the market, then begin with a new product. If it is what the new product can do, then begin with that.

Always include attribution in your lead. Who said it? Who developed the new process? The attribution could be a person or a company. If you're announcing quarterly earnings, you might attribute the company – "The ABC Company of Canada Ltd. today announced earnings of $3 million for the three months ended September 30, 1993."

If you're announcing a major capital program, you may want to give attribution to the President or some other senior executive – "The ABC Company of Canada Ltd. will spend $25 million to double the capacity of its widget plant in Everytown, John Smith, the company's president, announced today."

The rest of the news release should flow naturally from your lead, if you follow these rules:

- Back up your lead. If it makes an assertion – say, that your company's new widget is the most advanced of its kind – give supporting evidence. That may be a description of the new feature and how it compares to the existing widgets on the market, or it may be a quote from some authoritative source backing your assertion. You don't have to back up the lead right away. You may do this later on in the release if you need the intervening paragraphs to build up your argument.

- Sprinkle the release liberally with quotes. Direct quotes not only fix the source of what your saying, they also liven up the story. Quotes make a story more readable and more real. They bring the story closer to the reader, and they will increase the chances that your release will be used. Most editors and reporters like to use quotes and, of course, a direct quote, if it's used at all, must be used unchanged. A good quote, therefore, increases the odds that you'll get your message across in the media exactly the way you want to.

5. **There should be no loose ends.** The release should contain all the relevant facts, presented in logical sequence. A reporter may call you for more information. That's because you cannot anticipate everything the media might want to know. Even if you did, you

couldn't possibly fit all that information into one release. But you should not have any glaring holes or contradictions in the story. If you say there are five different types of widgets on the market, identify all of them, or none of them. Don't say: "Of the five, one is blue and another green." Everyone will want to know what the colours of the other three are. You may say: "The five types of widgets are identical, except for their colour. You can order them in any colour of the rainbow."

A good rule of thumb: Whatever information is needed to grasp the point you want the story to make should be included in your release. When talking about a possible strike, say how many workers are involved, and say whether you will continue to operate or shut down in the event of a work stoppage.

A second rule of thumb: If you haven't yet resolved an important question (such as staying open in the event of a strike) say so. "Mr. Smith said 'the company will announce its intentions following the union strike vote.' "

6. A news release should be held together by a central theme. You're firing a rifle, not a shotgun. Think of what you want to achieve with the release. Let's say your company is laying off 25 per cent of its workforce. You may have no choice but to announce that fact, so that will have to be the lead of your release. But your objective is not so much to let the world know of your impending move as it is to make your company look good. You want to turn a potentially harmful situation into a beneficial one.

So the theme running through the release might be that your company is on top of the major developments affecting your business and the economy as a whole, and that these developments require you to reduce costs and increase productivity. Only by improving your company's competitiveness can you ensure the long-term employment and prosperity of your remaining workforce.

To develop this theme, incorporate relevant background information and attitudes of senior executives into the release. Mention that the market for widgets has toughened, with prices declining as the result of growing competition. Back up this assertion by citing prices in actual dollars or the per cent by which they've fallen, then quote the president saying something along the lines of, "The layoffs, as painful as they might be to those affected, were necessary to secure the jobs of our other employees. We live in a highly competitive world, and our jobs and livelihoods depend on our ability to cut costs and increase productivity."

Then you might have the President saying something like, "We know we can meet this challenge, and I am confident that the ABC Widget Company will continue to be a world leader as a manufacturer of top-quality and competitively-priced widgets."

Finally, include the remaining points you listed at the beginning. These points may be facts that are not necessary to develop your theme, but might still be germane to the story. You can handle this quite simply by tagging them onto the end of the release: "The company also announced . . . ."

Releases Based on Speeches and Presentations

There are a few extra points to keep in mind when writing news releases based on speeches, submissions or other presentations.

1.   A news release is not an abridgement. You are not merely miniaturizing the speech or submission. Writing a news release, like writing a news story, is a process of selection. Your job is to choose the most salient points of the document and carefully select examples and quotes from it to illustrate those points.

2.   What is most important in the speech may not be the first thing mentioned on page one. The main point may often come in the middle or near the end, which means that you may find your lead somewhere on page 12 of a 17-page speech.

3.   Use lots of quotes – more than in other types of releases. After all, the story is what the speaker said, not your paraphrasing of what the speaker said.

4.   The story is not that John Smith spoke to the Ajax Rotary Club, it's what he said when speaking to the Ajax Rotary Club. So lead with what he said, following that with to whom he said it. Your lead might read, " 'Canadian-made widgets are the best thing since sliced bread,' John Smith, President of the Widget Company of Canada Ltd., today told the Ajax Rotary Club." Or if the lead contained more information, you might write it as follows:

   " 'Canadian-made widgets are the best thing since sliced bread and should become the country's biggest export item within five years,' John Smith, President of the Widget Company of Canada Ltd., said today.

"Mr. Smith told a luncheon meeting of the Ajax Rotary Club that his company's exports 'will enrich the Canadian economy by more than $100 million per year.' "

Here, secondary information, such as where Mr. Smith spoke, was relegated to the second paragraph by the pressure of more newsworthy and, from the company's point of view, more positive information.

To give the lead more actuality, use a direct quote if possible. If you can't quite find a phrase that fits, you might be able to paraphrase a sentence of the speech, putting one or two key words in quotes. Then, in succeeding paragraphs, you can develop Smith's idea in such a way as to fit in the full quote that uses the key words you selected for the lead.

IN BRIEF

What Makes a Story Newsworthy

- Relevance. Will the story have an impact on the daily lives of the people you are trying to reach?
- Topicality. Does the story deal with a major issue of the day or relate to a major holiday, event or person?
- Human interest. Does the story touch on an emotion or experience shared by most people?
- Entertainment value. Is the story funny or does it stimulate curiosity, imagination or passion?
- Controversy. The more outrageous or bitter the controversy, the more people want to see, hear and read about it.

The Media Information Kit

Possible Contents

1. A news release – the basic form of virtually all media communications.
2. Full texts of speeches or other documents, such as briefs, submissions or presentations upon which the news release is based.
3. "Fact sheets" giving relevant background to the issue or development you're publicizing.
4. A brochure or annual report that describes your company, agency or association.

5. Biographical sketches and glossy 5" by 7" or 8" by 10" black and white photographs of the key people mentioned in your release.

6. Covering letter to editors and reporters, inviting them to a news conference or interview.

How to Format a News Release

- Always double space text and print on only one side of a page.
- Put "For Immediate Release" or indicate release time at the top of the first page.
- Drop two lines and write a brief descriptive headline.
- Drop two lines and begin the news release text with a dateline, giving the city where the news is originating and the date.
- End all but the last page with the word "more" centred below the last line of text.
- Never end a page in the middle of a paragraph.
- Centre "-30-" below the last line of text.
- Put the name and phone numbers of the media contact person at the bottom of the last page.

Writing a News Release

1. Writing should be straightforward, lively and informative:
   - Avoid jargon. You're writing news, not a legal brief.
   - Write in active, not passive voice.
   - Write in the present tense only if the action described in the news release is not fixed to a particular event at a particular point in time. Otherwise use the past tense.
2. Organize your thoughts:
   - List all the points you want to make.
   - Prioritize the list.
3. Choose the content of your lead paragraph:
   - It must be near the top of your priority list.
   - It must be newsworthy.
4. Write the lead paragraph:
   - Incorporate as many of the five Ws – Who, What, When, Where and Why – as possible.
   - Attribute any assertions or announcements in the lead to a person or organization.

5. Back up the lead with supporting statements.
6. Sprinkle the release liberally with quotes.
7. Ensure there are no loose ends or logical inconsistencies.
8. Check to see that you've included all the important points on your priority list.

Telling Your Story To The Broadcast Media

10

While the fundamental principles and standards of good journalism apply equally to the print and broadcast media, each medium possesses unique qualities that may require special handling by the public relations practitioner.

What TV and Radio Reporters Need

Newspaper and magazine reporters primarily rely on the spoken or written word and first-hand or descriptive impressions of people and situations to write their stories. The print reporter doesn't have to be at the scene to write an interesting and informative account, although it certainly can help. Print reporters can work many of their stories over the phone, and even though their accounts might be enhanced by observations of the person being interviewed and of the physical surroundings, the liberal use of direct quotes will usually compensate. Nonetheless, when reporters are at the scene, they must observe and listen. And to do that, they must be close to where the action is.

Photographers, obviously, must be at the scene. But that's not enough. Being at the scene and holding a good vantage point may not necessarily be the same thing. What's the point of being at the location of an accident, if, amid the turmoil, all the photographer sees are the backs of the heads of rescue workers, onlookers or, worse yet, of reporters or other photographers. Photographers, therefore, insist on being first in line and will often shove, kick and gouge their way to the front, trying to displace reporters and other photographers who may already occupy that coveted position. But remember that the photographer can become the more desperate player. A reporter can arrive late and reconstruct events from interviews; a photographer cannot.

Radio reporters need "actuality" – the sounds of the event unfolding. That may be the plaintive cry of protesters chanting in the background to illustrate a political or social story. It may be the haunting call of a loon to set the stage for a feature on our threatened environment. It may be the voice of the prime ministerial candidate revelling in the joy of an election victory or struggling to maintain composed dignity through the anguish of defeat.

Or it may merely be the reporter speaking the story and thereby offering the listener the refreshing variety of hearing another voice. As a result, radio reporters are forever shoving microphones in people's faces. You can't do that from the back of the room or from the far end of the line, so radio reporters, like photographers, share a propensity to claw their way to centre stage.

TV reporters are like radio reporters, except that they have a camera crew in tow. And that sets them clearly apart from other media people. The addition of sight to the reporter's arsenal of words and sounds truly exacerbates the news-gathering process. Not only must the TV reporter be close to the centre of the action, but the accompanying camera crew and their sound and video equipment must be there, too. Having to integrate video with the written and recorded word further limits the flexibility of the TV journalist and makes it much more difficult to reconstruct stories from the newsroom. Without good video and good audio, the story will suffer immeasurably in the stiff competition for air time. So the TV journalist, especially the camera operator, will likely be more aggressive than journalists from other media in the battle for the preferred vantage point at the scene of fast-breaking news stories.

Running a News Conference

The situation that best illustrates the differences among the various media and the pitfalls into which the unwary practitioner may fall is the news conference. The growing use of the term "news" conference, as opposed to the more traditional "press" conference, represents recognition of the now firmly established position of radio and television in the media pantheon.

Unfortunately, recognition of the importance of the broadcast media does not necessarily translate into effective action. All too often, failure to accommodate the varying needs of the assembled media results in a chaotic news conference in which the focus of attention threatens to shift to often rude and occasionally violent exchanges between camera crew and photographer or reporter and photographer – with the hapless CEO at the podium fading angrily into the background.

Of course, this won't happen if you arrange your news conferences in such a way that you satisfy the basic needs of the print, radio and television journalists. You do this primarily by segmenting the room into functional compartments for each type of media.

- Sit the speaker at a table (or have the speaker stand at a podium) placed on a raised platform. This will give a good view to everyone in the room, especially the photographers and camera crews whose line of vision won't be blocked by reporters' heads.

- Provide "pool" boxes for high-quality audio feeds for both radio and TV people. This will eliminate the need for each individual radio and TV station to place a microphone on the podium or table. And it will ensure that late-arriving radio reporters or TV crews won't have to disrupt the proceedings as they add their microphone to an already overgrown bouquet.

- Put the feeds on tables that are set up along the sides of the room perpendicular to the speaker's table and on the floor just in front of where you place the TV camera crews.

- Leave plenty of space between the tables and the walls. This gives an area where photographers can work without getting in the way of reporters and camera crews.

- Complete the square by placing the video crews at the back of the room.

- Seat the reporters within the square. If possible, arrange the seats to avoid a centre aisle, since you don't want late-arriving (or early-departing) reporters walking up or down the centre of the room. But do leave space for an aisle between the ends of each row of chairs and the front of the audio feed tables.

- And, finally, provide lighting for the TV cameras. Professional lighting will help ensure high-quality video and thus increase the chances of a clip being used. It will also present a more attractive image of the person holding the news conference, since it will eliminate both the harsh shadows that are often produced by poor lighting and the need for the camera operator to use a head-on camera-mounted light that could irritate the eyes and cause the speaker to squint.

In addition to finely honed media relations skills, putting on a successful news conference also requires a high degree of technical knowledge and high-tech equipment. You must possess the skills, but if you don't have an encyclopaedic knowledge of the latest audio and video technology and your office doesn't own the most modern equipment, don't despair. You can rent both the expertise and the equipment.

One of Canada's leading experts in setting up news conferences is Burke Van Valkenburg. Most of what I know about the technical side of news conferences I learned from Burke. And he has another piece of advice that is worth heeding: If you have texts of remarks to be made at the news conference, hand them out beforehand to the camera operator. Video tapes run only for a maximum of 20 minutes, which means they will have to be changed at least once during the course of the average news conference. Ensuring that the camera operator has the text of opening remarks or speeches will greatly decrease the chance that your CEO will be in the middle of his key statement just when the camera runs out of tape.

And don't be led into complacency by the fact that those remarks only run five or 10 minutes and that, therefore, there will be plenty of time for all those immortal words on a 20-minute tape. TV stations just love to film the news conference leader entering the room. It gives them a bit of action in what might otherwise be a physically static situation. So by the time you get around to the prepared remarks, several precious minutes of that 20-minute tape will have been used up.

And this brings me to a couple of final points:

First, you, the PR person, should introduce the leader and then have him or her make an entrance, thus giving the TV people a chance for their action shot.

Second, hand out any written materials – texts of remarks, backgrounders, and so on – before the start of the news conference, not just to the camera operator but to all media people. I don't know how many times I've been told: "But if you give the reporters the text before the news conference, they'll have what they came for and they won't stick around."

Balderdash! If all the reporters needed was your written material, then you shouldn't have called the news conference in the first

Hey, what's going on here? Reporters, photographers and camera crew battle each other and a barrage of microphones to get to the members of the Green Ribbon Task force after the arrest of Paul Bernardo.

Photo courtesy of Canapress Photo Service

place. You could simply have delivered the material directly to the reporters in their respective newsrooms and saved them the trouble of traipsing down to your useless event. Giving reporters the text merely makes their job easier. Most reporters will wish to check the prepared text against delivery to ensure that they quote what the news conference leader actually said, not merely what was intended to be said. And that job can't be done effectively unless the reporters have the text in front of them while the words are being spoken.

Giving out the text also increases the odds that your story will be told the way you want it to. Even if a reporter or two leaves early, with the text tucked under their arms, so what? The text contains your story told the way you want it told, and if a reporter is content to use that and that alone, so much the better for you.

Here's how the news conference ought to be set up. There's one microphone for each speaker and audio feed boxes at the side tables for radio or print reporters who want to record the proceedings. The head table is on a raiser to permit an unobstructed view for video cameras, which will be stationed at the rear of the room. Notice, too, the audio feed box on the floor for the television crews.

A well-run news conference in action. Everyone's in place and there's a place for everyone.

Using the Same Release for Print and Broadcast Media

I am frequently asked whether you should send the same news release to the print and broadcast media. The basis for the question is that radio and television need very brief news items. If a five-minute hourly radio newscast is to contain, say 10 items, with an average of only 30 seconds for each, that translates into about 80 to 100 words – far fewer than the average news release, which runs about 300 words. Naturally, the question arises: "Should I send a 300-word news release to the newspapers and a 90-word news release to radio and television?"

In most cases, the answer is "no." If you've written the news releases properly in the first place, the first paragraph or two – that is, the first 20 to 50 words – should tell the story in such a way that the release meets the basic requirements of good journalism and covers the essential points that your organization wants to make. Indeed, if you were to send a separate news release to radio or television, that news release, ideally, would be the first two paragraphs of the news release you sent to the newspapers.

But there may be exceptions. If the story is complex and multi-faceted and can be expected to continue to develop over a period of time – such as during a really hot crisis – you may want to provide the radio stations with a package of half a dozen or so 15-second or 30-second news briefs. Each one of the briefs can then be used on successive hourly news broadcasts. The stations are happy because each broadcast will contain a new angle on the story, and you're happy because each of the news briefs contains one of your key points and your story is the one being told. If you distribute such a package, be sure to include backgrounders, fact sheets or other material to support the statements made in the briefs.

The Video News Release (VNR)

The video news release is one of the newest tools available to corporations, trade and professional associations, government agencies and political parties that have a story to tell or a message to deliver. It is also one of the most controversial and least understood weapons in the communicator's arsenal.

Since they burst on the North American scene more than a decade ago, video news releases have been subjected equally to harsh criticism and high praise. Their detractors point to high cost and low pickup rates by TV stations. Their supporters cite more positive treatment and wider exposure for your story than can normally be achieved by the "traditional" written news release.

Both sides are right. VNRs are expensive. Production and distribution of a bare-bones 90-second video news release will cost a minimum of $5,000, with the price rising to between $10,000 and $20,000 for one of good quality and longer duration.

What do you get for all that money? And are the benefits worth the cost?

First, you have to understand that a video news release is, truly, a news release, and to be an effective communications tool it must meet the same criteria of newsworthiness and professionalism as any written news release.

The essential difference between a written and video news release is that with the latter you are packaging your message in a form that is tailored to the specific needs of a particular medium – you are giving a video to a medium that specializes in video. So to be successful, your VNR must not only meet high journalistic standards and not only deal with a newsworthy subject, it must also be visually appealing and of high technical video and audio quality. If your VNR meets all these criteria, it stands a good chance of being used by a significant number of TV stations.

When to Use a VNR

Before I go any further, I have a confession to make – I have never done a video news release. So I have no first-hand knowledge of the difficulty of production, the agony of getting internal approval for, and then maintaining, budgets, the various methods of distribution or the means at hand for evaluating the success or failure of a VNR program. What I know, I have learned from others or divined from examining others' VNRs and the coverage they received.

From that, it's clear that there are times when VNRs can be the most appropriate means of getting the message across.

With Unique Events   One very successful VNR consisted of footage of two hang-glider experts diving off Toronto's CN Tower. It was picked up by the networks as well as a host of independent stations. Why? First, because the visuals were excellent – a video camera mounted on the back of one of the divers gave a thrilling bird's-eye view of the flight. Second, the subject itself had tremendous human interest appeal. It was a daredevil stunt, replete with drama, danger and determination. And third, it would have been impossible for more than one station to film the event. After all, how many cameras can you strap to the back of a hang-glider pilot? A traditional news release would have excited extensive newspaper interest, but it would not have produced as widespread TV coverage as that generated by a well-planned and well-executed video news release.

As Features Video news releases are ideally suited for feature stories that can be planned well in advance. The more time you can spend scripting, shooting and editing the VNR, the better it will be. And the more time the station has to schedule and air the story, the greater the chance that it will be picked up. The launch of new products or services and the celebration or marking of such events as a company's diamond jubilee, the dismantling of the Berlin Wall or the 50th anniversary of the invention of the nylon stocking could each be the subject of an excellent VNR.

With Fast Breaking News The same holds true of some breaking news stories. The chairman's remarks at the company's annual meeting would qualify if he or she were discussing major corporate activities of wide interest to the business community or consumers, or making pithy and insightful remarks about the general health of the economy or other issues of broad public interest.

In Crisis Situations It might also be beneficial to issue a video news release in certain crisis situations. In the late 1980s, Gillette came under attack by animal rights advocates who claimed that rabbits were being mistreated in the company's research laboratories. The company, which knew that a demonstration was going to be held at a divisional office in Toronto, produced a VNR of Dr. Robert Giovacchini, the vice-president of product integrity, denying that animals were abused and explaining the reasons for testing products on laboratory animals before they were sold to humans. The idea was to encourage TV stations covering the demonstration to include the company's views in their report – and it worked. Of three TV news clips that I saw, two used key sections of the VNR; in the third, the reporter encapsulated what Dr. Giovacchini said in the video.

Instead of producing a video news release, Dr. Giovacchini could have chosen to make himself available for TV interviews. Making the right choice involves correctly answering several key questions: Would more stations free up a crew to conduct an interview than would use a well-prepared video news release? If demand for interviews were high, would Dr. Giovacchini be available to give them all? Would you want TV crews wandering in and out of your office or plant? How effectively would Dr. Giovacchini get the company's views across in possibly hostile interviews?

My judgement is that Gillette was wise to produce a video news release in this situation. Dr. Giovacchini is based in the United States. Of course, he could have come to Toronto to give the interviews. But I'm sure that most stations would have insisted that the interview take place at the demonstration site. This would raise the prospect of a confrontation with the demonstrators – a welcome development for the media, but a potentially disastrous one for Gillette. Dr. Giovacchini was wise to stay out of harm's way.

When VNRs May Not Be Appropriate

VNRs are not appropriate in all situations that may be newsworthy or provide good visual opportunities. In the summer of 1986, for example, the Cathedral of the Transfiguration in Markham, just north of Toronto, invited the media to attend the blessing of a new peal of bells that were about to be hoisted into the Cathedral's three spires. This was a great visual story, but we did not produce a VNR. Instead, a media kit containing a covering letter, news release and several fact sheets was sent to the media several days prior to the event (see page 92). The material described what was going to happen in sufficient detail for the TV news directors to send their own crews to cover the event, and the story was broadcast on virtually all independent and network stations in the Metro Toronto area.

A VNR might have produced slightly greater TV coverage, especially by independent stations in other parts of the country. But would that added coverage have been worth the expense of a VNR? I didn't think so. The Cathedral's objective was to gain greater public understanding of, and support for the Cathedral and the Byzantine Rite of the Catholic Church. But it does not have a large PR budget. Spending $5,000 to $10,000 on a VNR might have marginally increased TV coverage of the hoisting of the bells, but it would have depleted (if not exceeded) the communications budget. We would have ended up with only one kick at the can – albeit a good kick – with no means to conduct follow-up activities. That's like spending a fortune to produce a beautiful and persuasive magazine ad and then running it only once. It will make a big but soon-to-be-forgotten splash that will have minimal lasting benefit.

You should know what sets television apart from the other media and you should know how to accommodate the special requirements of TV news. But, most importantly, you must be able to determine the most efficient and beneficial use of your limited financial and human resources. You must decide whether spending the money for a VNR to increase TV coverage of a particular event is more productive than spending the money on other aspects of your public relations program. After all is said and done, TV news may not be the most cost-efficient way to reach your targeted audiences. But then again, it may be.

Risky Business: Planting Your Story   11

I have no way of knowing for sure, but I suspect that most of the celebrated scandals of recent memory – from the Watergate debacle to Jim Bakker's sexual indiscretion – would never have come to light without a willing informer who initially piqued the media's interest with a tantalizing morsel of gossip and then supplied selected reporters with ever-juicier bits of information.

The Watergate break-in would have gone down in history as a simple burglary with little or no political overtones if it had not been for Deep Throat, a still-anonymous informer. And I doubt very much that the *Miami Herald* reporters would have been staking out Gary Hart's Washington townhouse during the 1988 US presidential primary election campaign if they had not received an anonymous tip that the presidential hopeful was planning to have company that night.

The fact is, most information can be kept secret if the people who possess that information want it to be kept secret. The danger, of course, is that people talk, sometimes willingly, sometimes not, but usually with the same result – the cat gets out of the bag.

In earlier chapters, I cast the media relations practitioner in the role of victim – the one about whom information may be inadvertently publicized – and advised preemptive action with the admonition that if you don't tell your story, someone else may tell it for you, and get it wrong.

The ensuing discussion referred solely to open and public distribution of your story to the media. You had a story to tell, so you told it. There was no doubt in the minds of the media or the general public what the story was or where it came from. And that's the way it ought to be, most of the time. But there are times – and they should only be few and far between – when you may not want the public to know where the story came from, but you do want the story published.

So it becomes your turn to play tattletale and plant your nugget of news in the hope that it will grow into a full-fledged story, in much the same way that a gardener plants seeds in the hope that Mother Nature, using her own devices, will produce an ear of corn or a pod of peas. But just as a late frost, insect infestation or the bone-burying penchant of the neighbour's dog can ruin a garden, unforeseen developments can kill your planted story before it ever breaks ground. To make your task even more difficult, you may have to use your skills not only to keep your seedling planted story alive, but also to make sure that it doesn't assume a life of its own and, like an unweeded garden, grow out of control.

Because of the risks, planting a story should be a last resort. You turn to it only when it is imperative that your story be told, and imperative that you are not linked to the telling of the story.

How to Proceed When It's Absolutely Necessary

Here's a case in point. Your company is bidding on a lucrative government contract. Details of the bids and decision-making process would not normally be publicized or be of much interest to the media. In this instance, however, your company is taking an innovative approach that will greatly benefit the public. But your proposal varies from the criteria established by the government when asking for tenders and, therefore, may not win approval. You feel that media coverage may stimulate public debate, which, in turn, will give your proposal a better chance of acceptance. On the downside, however, you know that the government will not like your going to the media, and you are understandably concerned that doing so may cost you the contract. This is a no-win situation. You keep quiet, you lose the contract. You go to the media, you lose the contract.

A way out of the dilemma in this situation may be to don your cloak and dagger and plant the story. Your goal is to get the story published without the government suspecting – or at least knowing for sure – that it came from you. If you are successful, you will generate public debate on your proposal without getting the government mad at you.

That, of course, may be easier said than done. The reality is that there are no guarantees of success. But as with other aspects of media relations, you can minimize your risk and maximize your control over the situation. The only difference here is that the risks are greater and the potential for control less than in other media situations.

Given these caveats, here's how to proceed.

Select the Approach   First, decide whether to go to the media directly with your story or to keep your involvement secret even from the media. The former approach is much simpler, much quicker and gives you greater control over the final story. The risk is that the reporter you speak to will not maintain your anonymity.

The situation is reversed with the latter approach. You have a better chance of remaining anonymous, but you have much less control over what the final story – if it ever appears – will say. And the process of developing the story could take much longer.

In the example of the government contract, you will probably have to go directly to the media. Time is an important consideration. The story has got to be published before the government decides which proposal to use. You want the story to describe the particular innovations of your company's proposal and how they will benefit the general public. The best way to achieve this is to set yourself up as a media contact – either to give information or to tell the reporter where to get the information.

Your challenge is to identify the most effective media outlet or outlets for your story. Things to consider are the publics reached by the various media, their credibility with those publics and their general responsiveness to planted stories. Knowing just the right editor or reporter to approach is equally important. Your contact must not only be trustworthy, he or she must be a good journalist. There is no sense in planting a story if the reporter is going to get it wrong. This is where getting to know the reporters who cover the activities of your organization pays off.

Approach the Media   Your next challenge is to approach the media. I suppose there are people out there who could charm the spots off a leopard, but I'm not one of them. I would never have made it as a con man – and for the vast majority of you who share this "shortcoming," I would suggest you not try to pull a fast one. If you're planting a story, say so, and explain your reasons. If they are legitimate, you should have no difficulty. If they are not, then you should not be planting the story in the first place, or at least you should have taken a much more surreptitious approach to begin with.

And finally, once you've contacted the media, establish the ground rules. I have repeatedly warned that nothing is off the record; everything you tell a reporter can be published or broadcast. But this doesn't mean you can't make a deal with a reporter before you start talking. You may, for example, agree to be interviewed on condition that your name and affiliation be kept secret. If the reporter believes you've got a good story, your chances of reaching agreement are pretty good. After all, reporters thrive on inside information. More dirt is spread by disgruntled employees, spurned business partners or ambitious executives who will eagerly tell the most sacred secret in exchange for a promise of anonymity than by any bulldozer yet invented. Just ask Jim Bakker, or Richard Nixon. But remember, your deal with the reporter doesn't change the fact that what you say will be reported. It merely stipulates how that information will be credited.

Protect Yourself   And this brings you to the most challenging part of the exercise – how to present the information in such a way that it will not be traced back to you. Simply giving the facts anonymously may not be good enough. It may protect your anonymity, but it may not hide the fact that your organization initiated the story. In the case of the company vying for a government contract, that won't do.

The most effective solution would be to give details of the proposals made by the other companies vying for the contract. This way the story would not just be about you and the information it contained would point to the other companies or perhaps even the government agency itself as the source. Then again, you may not have the details of the other proposals – after all, they were given in secret to the government just as yours was.

The next best bet is to give the names of the other companies bidding for the contract and hope that the reporter will ferret out sufficient information to draw attention away from you. Your only hope here is that the other companies may share your desire for publicity.

Of course, in the end, the story may contain only your unattributed comments, leaving you with at least one foot in the doghouse.

As I said, planting stories can be a risky business.

Brown Bagging It

There are similar risks with the indirect approach; that is, keeping your identity secret from the media as well as from the public. You could, for example, "brown bag" your story – anonymously delivering a telltale document to your selected reporter. As a cloak-and-dagger variant on this theme, you could arrange an interview with the reporter on another subject entirely, and, with the evidence placed conspicuously on your desk, leave the room for a few minutes. You never know, the technique may work. Even though your company might be traced as the source of the information, company officials might only be accused of carelessness, not complicity in the planting of the story. Of course, this, in itself, may be damning enough to cost your company the contract.

As a final resort, you could spread your story by rumour. Casually mention between drinks at the press club that the government is unusually concerned about avoiding media coverage of the tendering process for that big government contract. The ensuing speculation that someone has got something to hide might eventually get an enterprising reporter to phone the various companies making the proposals or the government agency issuing the contract in search of answers. And where it goes from there is anybody's guess. The trouble with cranking up the rumour mill is that it may then be impossible to gear it down again.

Frankly, I think the risks associated with this clandestine side of journalism are too great to take in any but the most compelling circumstances.

What To Do When The Media Get It Wrong

It is inevitable that sooner or later, despite your best efforts news accounts will contain errors that put your organization in a bad light.

You may have initiated the stories yourself through a proactive media program, with the error or distortion resulting from poor reporting or editing. You may have been interviewed at the initiation of the reporter. Or the story may have been written without the reporter ever having contacted you. The errors of fact or emphasis may have been the result of an honest misunderstanding by the reporters or editors working on the story, the unconscious expression of bias or a manifestation of deliberate manipulation of the truth.

In any event, do your swearing and indignant desk-pounding in the privacy of your office. Ranting and raving to the reporter or editor won't help you, and neither will inaction spawned by a belief that you are powerless to right the wrongs perpetrated by the media. Brooding over the shortcomings of the media will do nothing towards getting the media to publish or broadcast positive items about you.

In fact, errors of commission or omission by the media frequently present opportunities for you to get favourable coverage by the offending publication. Being the victim of media wrongdoing puts you in the driver's seat. You can negotiate a remedy from strength as you press to have your story told correctly or claim limited space in the publication to tell your story yourself.

Be Sure You Have a Legitimate Gripe

I always examine my clients' media coverage to ensure that it was accurate and balanced. I will occasionally go a step further and scrutinize stories in search of errors, omissions or biases that can serve as pegs for some type of positive corrective follow-up. I will rarely let harmful errors or biases go unanswered.

The purpose of these exercises is not to harass the media or wreak vengeance on an unfriendly reporter. It is to ensure that my client's story is told fairly and comprehensively. It is part of the on-going process of evaluating my client's goals and objectives, isolating those aspects of the client's activities or achievements that would occasion beneficial media coverage, then identifying the publics to whom I want to tell my story and the media that can best tell it to them.

Prior to taking any action on an inaccurate or unfavourable story, however, make sure you carefully analyze what was really wrong with it.

- Were any facts wrong? If so, make sure you have the correct information and can verify it.

- Were the facts contained in the story correct, but the overall impression inaccurate because other relevant facts were omitted? If so, get those missing facts, show their relevance and be able to explain clearly and simply how the impression given by the story was wrong.

- Did certain words used by the reporter convey an unfair impression? Some words are emotionally charged, or carry pejorative connotations. If so, be able to prove your case. Descriptive terms such as "oily," "shifty" or "grasping" clearly convey a negative impression, and if they were used you would certainly have a grievance, possibly even grounds for a libel action. But you're more likely to see descriptives that are unflattering rather than libelous, such as "rotund," "unkempt" or "haggard." The question is, are these descriptions accurate, and if accurate, was it appropriate to use them?

If, for any of these reasons, a story about you or your organization creates a false and harmful impression, you should take action. But beware of a major pitfall. A story may be harmful to you, but be neither inaccurate nor biased. The fact is, you may have deserved the negative publicity. In that case, complaining does you little good.

As the Reuters correspondent in Denmark during the first oil crisis back in the early 1970s, I was tipped off about remarks that the

Danish Prime Minister had just made at a political meeting in a small industrial city outside Copenhagen.

Denmark, like other industrial countries, was being threatened with oil sanctions by the Arab countries, which were trying to pressure the West into withdrawing its support for Israel. In this heated environment, the Prime Minister, when asked about events in the Middle East, took Israel's side and said the Arabs were trying to push Israel into the sea. If, indeed, the Prime Minister said what he was reported to have said, this was news.

To check out the facts before filing my story to Reuters, I got a copy of the account written by the local stringer who had attended the meeting on behalf of the Danish news agency. I called the reporter to verify his story and to ask a few questions of my own. I couldn't get hold of the Prime Minister at his office or home, but I left urgent messages. I then tried to reach his executive assistant, with the same negative result. To be on the safe side, I waited a couple of hours before writing my story, to give the Prime Minister or his staff a chance to return my call. They never did.

The next day, after my Reuters story was picked up by the media in most of the Arab countries – which condemned the Prime Minister for supporting Israel and called for even heavier sanctions against his country – I got an urgent call from a very distraught and accusatory prime ministerial assistant.

He demanded that I correct my "erroneous" story. But where were the errors? I read the account of the Prime Minister's statement I got from the Danish reporter. The assistant acknowledged that the statement was accurate. I read him my English translation. Yep, that was okay, too.

"Then what's wrong with the story?" I asked.

"The Prime Minister's remarks were reported out of context. He didn't make them in a prepared statement, but in response to a question from the audience."

I read him my story, which, indeed, had the Prime Minister making his remarks in response to a question. In the end, the assistant conceded that the story was both truthful and accurate.

The real problem here was not with the story, but with the Prime Minister. If he didn't want to be quoted as saying what he said, he should have kept his mouth shut. And he should not have tried to make a scapegoat out of the reporter.

What Are Your Options?

If you've analyzed a negative story about you and feel you have a legitimate gripe, the next step is to decide how the error should be rectified to your best advantage.

You have several options. The most common are either to get the publication to print a correction or clarification or to write a letter to the editor. But there are also other, less commonly used, avenues open to you.

One is to write a guest column under your byline for the "op-ed" page of the paper, if it has one. This is a page, usually opposite the editorial page (thus the name), that is reserved for outside commentators. Another possible course of action is to suggest a catchy angle for another article that would present your story in a more balanced and enlightened way.

And if the published or broadcast errors about you or your organization are so widespread and harmful that you feel these tools – correction, letter to the editor, op-ed page article or follow-up story by a single publication – would make too little an impression, you can always launch a media program of your own. Nothing prevents you from issuing a news release, calling a news conference, arranging media interviews or appearing on talk shows to set the record straight about erroneous media coverage, provided the issue is of sufficient public interest. Biased or inaccurate reporting can, itself, become newsworthy. CTV, for example, took the *Toronto Star* to task for what the network regarded as biased coverage of the Canada-US free trade debate. Ironically, Beland Honderich, publisher of the *Star*, like so many other corporate heads pursued by the media, refused to be interviewed.

As a last resort, you could also make a complaint to the Press Council in your province or bring a civil suit against the publication, its senior editors and the reporters and copy editors who worked on the story.

Setting the Record Straight in the Print Media

So how do you go about it? If a newspaper or magazine published an incorrect identification or description of a key individual in your organization or of a product or service provided by your organization, or if it disseminated false information that might have a material effect on the fortunes of the company (say, misquoting a profit or loss), then you'll want the record set straight.

It's especially important to do that with the print media because in the future other reporters will likely refer to that original news item when researching their own stories. An incorrect fact or assertion is thus likely to be repeated time and time again. So insist on a correction or clarification.

Correction and Clarification   If a story is unbalanced, incomplete or biased, a correction or clarification may not be the most effective remedy. Corrections and clarifications are brief, in most cases no longer than a single paragraph, and this will rarely be enough space to set the record straight on a story whose very structure was invalid. (A clarification is very much like a correction, except that in a clarification, the publication is saying only that the information it published was unclear, not incorrect.)

If your local paper published an article describing how industrial sulphur dioxide emissions are destroying the environment, but failed to mention that many companies, including your own, have spent millions of dollars to cut emissions, for example, a correction or clarification would merely say that such-and-such article did not mention that your company or your industry spent X million dollars last year on sulphur dioxide emission control.

That may be fine, as far as it goes. But by using the other remedies available to you, you could greatly enhance the opportunities for getting substantial, positive exposure and thereby bring your organization that much closer to achieving its overall communications objectives.

Whatever your grievance, don't go over the reporter's head to the editor, news director or publisher. Call the reporter first and calmly explain what was wrong with the story. The reporter will do one of four things:

1. Admit he made a mistake and ask whether you want a correction printed.

2. Agree that there was an error that he would like to rectify in a follow-up story.

3. Agree that the story may not have been entirely accurate or balanced, but maintain that no follow-up or correction is warranted.

4. Dispute that the story was erroneous or distorted, as I did with the Prime Minister's assistant.

If you resolve the issue with the reporter, then that's the end of it. If you can't agree on a solution with the reporter, however, then you may want to take the matter up with the reporter's editor to argue for a correction, or you may simply want to write a letter to the editor.

For all practical purposes, daily newspapers run on a 24-hour cycle. So even if there was an urgent need to get something corrected at the earliest opportunity, you would have several hours to analyze the situation and prepare your response. Then you would have to wait until the next day before the situation was rectified. In most cases, you would actually have considerably more time – often as much as two or three days, depending on the type of remedy you're seeking – in preparing your response. Then you might have to wait another day or two before anything appeared in print.

A correction should be published the next day, if possible. A letter to the editor or an op-ed page article can wait longer. The basic reason is that a correction is brief. There is virtually no opportunity in the four, five or six lines of a correction to provide the readers with background material to jog their memory about the original story. Being substantially longer, letters to the editor and commentaries give you ample opportunity to develop a line of thought and provide information that can really stand independently from the original story.

Whatever you decide, tell the reporter what your intentions are. If you are going to call the reporter's editor to complain and ask for a correction or clarification, say so. The reporter will respect your directness and fairness.

If you do decide to call the editor, confine your remarks to the merits of the story, not the merits of the reporter. Attacking the reporter will merely put the editor on the defensive. Chances are, if your case is valid, the editor will be accommodating. If not, a letter to the editor may be your best option.

Letter to the Editor   The letters page can be a good forum for your views, so don't be afraid to use it. But stick to the facts. Keep the letter short. Rarely will a newspaper publish a letter that runs more than 300 words.

The tone of the letter can be firm, and you should point out the specific shortcomings of the article, citing possible factual errors, distortions or sloppy research. But the letter should not be personal or vindictive. You may indict the reporter for not calling you to check out a fact, but don't call the reporter stupid or incompetent.

Remember, you're not out to get the reporter, you're out to correct a harmful impression given of your organization. You're out to make friends, not enemies. So don't vent your spleen. You'll appear petulant, foolish or immature. If you represent a large company, you'll seem like a bully, too. A well-balanced letter to the editor is an effective communications tool, and it will be appreciated, just as you appreciate a well-balanced news article about your company.

Last Resorts If the newspaper does not publish your letter, or if your letter is so heavily edited that the points you wanted to raise are obscured, you could take your grievance to the Press Council. And if that route fails and you believe the error was libelous or otherwise threatened the well-being of your organization, you can always call your lawyer for advice on possible legal action.

Recognizing an Opportunity

Keep uppermost in your mind that an error of fact, a palpable bias, a lack of balance or a significant omission in a news story can serve as an opportunity, not only to set the record straight, but also to repeat important information or reinforce attitudes and perceptions.

I was once retained by John Hasek, a retired army major, to help publicize his campaign for school trustee in a Toronto by-election. Mr. Hasek held strong views on the harm that was being caused by what he regarded as the introduction of partisan politics to the Board of Education and by the propounding of political ideology in the classroom. He was running in a large field, which included some highly experienced politicians who tried to undermine Mr. Hasek's credibility by presenting him as a right-wing extremist.

I believed it was imperative that the electorate saw Mr. Hasek for what he was: A concerned citizen who wanted to ensure that the public school system properly prepared our children for a productive and fulfilling adulthood. So Mr. Hasek did all the usual things to generate media coverage: He gave interviews, held news conferences, distributed news releases and invited the media to attend all-candidates meetings.

Then I scrutinized the coverage, in hopes of finding yet another peg upon which to generate even more media coverage. Among the things I was searching for were factual errors, distortions or omissions upon which to base a letter to the editor. In effect, I wanted a forum in which Mr. Hasek could present himself and his election platform in a clear, concise and unedited way. I was seeking an opportunity for Mr. Hasek to counter the unwarranted attacks on him by demonstrating that he was sincere and informed and would be an effective advocate for good education.

The media coverage of the campaign was surprisingly extensive, with news and feature stories appearing regularly in all three Toronto dailies. For the most part, that coverage was fair and balanced. But the newspapers can report only so much. The competition for limited space among a host of other important stories of the day meant, quite naturally and expectedly, that the specifics of Mr. Hasek's campaign platform would not be reported in anywhere near the depth that we regarded as necessary.

To get our full story out required another platform – the letters page of the *Toronto Star*. I was offered two opportunities. The first was a feature in the *Sunday Star*. It was a balanced report, with which I could find no fault. The headline, however, referred to John Hasek as a "militarist." That's an emotionally charged word that carries a well-deserved negative connotation. It was also an inaccurate description of the candidate. He might have been a career officer in the Armed Forces, but that did not make him a militarist, which my Webster's defines as someone who advocates "predominance of the military class or its ideals."

That characterization could have provided the peg for a letter to the editor, which would have outlined what Mr. Hasek did, in fact, stand for. Doing this, however, would have required repetition of the offending characterization. I still believed that the benefits of a well-crafted letter to the editor would have outweighed the disadvantages of repeating the reference to Mr. Hasek as a militarist, but I would have preferred another option.

Luckily, one emerged two days later. It was the statement in an otherwise accurate account of an all-candidates meeting that John Hasek "also told the largely hostile audience at St. Paul's Centre at Trinity he is opposed to sex education in the schools."

Mr. Hasek did not say he opposed sex education; he said he opposed the advocacy of any particular lifestyle as part of the sex education program. This was the opportunity I was looking for, and as soon as the error was brought to my attention, I wrote a letter to the editor for Mr. Hasek to sign.

I then called the reporter, who readily conceded that her story contained that one error. I suggested a letter to the editor as a remedy and read her the draft I had written. She had no problem with it, and suggested that I discuss the matter further with Rod Goodman, the newspaper's Ombudsman. To facilitate matters, she volunteered to let him know of the situation. This she did, and when I phoned Mr. Goodman the next day, he agreed to discuss the letter with Pat Whittaker, editor of the Letters-to-the-Editor page. Ms. Whittaker's only concern was that the letter, which ran 300 words, dealt with Mr. Hasek's entire platform and not just the issue of sex education but, in the end, she agreed to publish it in full, in the interests of fairness on the eve of an election.

And here's the letter as published:

Candidate advocates sex education

School board elections generally excite very little interest among the voters, a highly unfortunate situation given the importance of education for any generation of Canadians and the depth of the problems now facing our school system. For this reason, The Star deserves credit for the extensive coverage it is giving to the Oct. 29 by-election for school trustee in Toronto's Ward 5.

That coverage has, for the most part, been balanced and comprehensive. But in an otherwise accurate account of an all-candidates meeting at St. Paul's Centre (Classroom not the place for teachers' opinions, Ward 5 candidate says, Oct. 19), the account of my views on sex education in the schools was incorrect.

I believe that sex education, like other subjects that are important to the process of preparing our children for adulthood, has a definite place in our schools.

What I told the all-candidates meeting, and what I have been saying throughout the campaign, is that teachers should not be advocating any particular lifestyle when conducting classes on sex education, just as they should not be advocating any particular ideology when teaching history or current affairs.

Every individual makes choices about his or her own lifestyle and politics. But as teachers or members of the school board, we must recognize that schools cannot prepare our children to lead fulfilling and productive lives and to be responsible members of our democratic society through indoctrination either in lifestyle or political orientation.

They can do it only by teaching the basic academic skills of reading, writing, mathematics, by offering comprehensive physical education programs, by instilling an appreciation of the arts, and by imparting a knowledge of such other subjects as history, geography, current affairs, French and, indeed, human sexuality.

This is what I advocate. And this is the basic issue of the by-election.

JOHN HASEK
Candidate for School Trustee
Ward 5, Toronto

The *Star* may have its faults, but its dedication to factual reporting is second to none. The position of Ombudsman is no empty public relations gesture; it is an expression of a deep commitment to the highest ideals of good journalism. But, to be truly effective, this commitment and dedication must also be shared by readers – and that includes the media relations specialist.

Ferret out the errors and inaccuracies in the coverage of your company, agency or association, then use your skills as a communicator to get your message across, factually and comprehensively. If you don't use every legitimate means at your disposal to tell your story, then the media cannot possibly fulfill their obligation to keep the public fully informed of important events.

You won't always succeed in getting a newspaper to correct what you may regard as incorrect or misleading information, but you will always fail if you don't try.

Unfortunately, in the case of John Hasek, we succeeded with the *Star*, but lost with the electorate.

Setting the Record Straight on Radio and Television

Erroneous, biased or unbalanced coverage is a problem with the broadcast as well as with the print media. The opportunities that these occurrences present and the procedures you should follow in dealing with them are similar. There are, however, important differences that will affect what you should do, how you should do it and when you should do it.

The fundamental difference between the print and broadcast media involves space and time.

"Space" is an interesting concept. With the print media, space has a nice, easy-to-grasp, two-dimensional quality – it's the physical area taken up by words on a page. With the broadcast media, words are not expressed spatially. Words do not occupy a physical area, they occupy time.

This difference affects the way people absorb news from the various media and the way those media present the news. Because a newspaper is a physical entity you, the reader, can pick and choose what you want to read and when you want to read it. Some people peruse the entire newspaper, just glancing at the headlines, others turn immediately to their favourite section or columnist, still others merely read the ads.

A newspaper is a potpourri of information, writing styles, attitudes and opportunities. While newspapers generally gear their coverage and style to certain socioeconomic groups, there is tremendous room for latitude – you can read those sections of the newspaper in any sequence you like, any time you like, omitting what doesn't interest you. Not every reader need share the same interests with all other readers. You can still hate sports and like the *Globe and Mail*. You simply skip over the sports section to get to the *Report on Business*.

The broadcast media don't work that way. If you don't like what's on the air at that particular moment, you can't flip to another news item. You can flip to another station or switch the set off, but the original station will have lost you. The broadcast media have to hold the attention of their audience with much greater tenacity than do the print media. Consequently, they have much less latitude in their selection of the news items they cover and how they cover them. To hold audience attention, each radio or television news item must have broader appeal than the individual news items published in the daily newspaper.

The broadcast media are also bound by time. Assuming the newscaster speaks at a rate of 125 words per minute, there's room for only 1,875 words in each five-minute broadcast. That's equivalent to about four average-length newspaper stories, which for a major daily represents no more than about five per cent of the news hole. Newspapers have a lot more space than radio or TV stations have time.

What's more, you, the listener, must be tuned in when the radio or television station broadcasts an item or you miss it. To make sure that they reach as wide an audience as possible with each message – whether it be news or advertising – the broadcast media do a lot of repeating, further limiting the time available for fresh material. Tape recorders and VCRs are making the broadcast media more like newspapers as far as the time factor is concerned, but so far, at least, I don't believe significant numbers of people record radio or television news to play back at their leisure.

The time and space constraints under which the broadcast media operate will influence all of your dealings with them, especially when it comes to correcting news stories about you or your organization.

As noted before, newspapers operate on a 24-hour cycle. The time between learning of an error and getting it corrected is much shorter with the broadcast media, especially radio, where five-minute newscasts every half hour are not uncommon. Even if you wait only a few hours following a broadcast to contact the radio station about erroneous or unbalanced coverage, as many as a dozen newscasts may have transpired since the offending item was first aired. There's a risk that the error or distortion will be repeated in all or some of the intervening broadcasts. Each half hour you delay may serve only to increase the exposure given to the damaging news report.

The Range of Remedies

I once asked several radio and television news directors about their station's policy and procedures regarding erroneous, biased or unbalanced coverage. Their replies contained a lot of valuable information and a number of useful tips for the media relations practitioner.

Number one on their list of advice is to respond quickly to erroneous coverage. As John McFadyen, News Director of Toronto AM station CFRB, said, "if there is an error in fact, the radio station should be contacted as quickly as possible in order to avoid repetition of that error .... Because of the frequency and, therefore, quick turnover in radio news, there is nothing to be gained by delay."

The same goes for questions of balance in a story. But here McFadyen added another wrinkle. "Before making the call to question the balance or to add an angle, side or opinion to what has earlier been published," he advised, "the caller should expect to be asked to enunciate that opinion or concern during the telephone call." In other words, he added, "be prepared to be taped, and be prepared to be quoted when phone calls questioning balance are made."

The lesson here is simple: The error made by the media offers you an opportunity to tell your story in your own way, making the points that you want to make – the points that will help your organization achieve its goals and objectives.

The thinking that goes into getting an item corrected, therefore, is basically the same thinking that goes into the development of any media initiative. And this holds true for the print as well as the broadcast media.

Martin Vanderwoude, News Director at CKBB-FM in Barrie, Ontario, made another observation. "Radio," he suggested, "is probably a good way to correct statements made in newspapers, because they can be corrected instantly. Once a paper is out, it's out, but a radio news story can be changed almost hourly."

He illustrated this point with an anecdote about the local Hyundai dealer, who effectively used the broadcast media to counter an incorrect report published in the Toronto newspapers and carried by the broadcast news wire.

As Vanderwoude told the story, the newspapers reported that Hyundai Motor Company officials said they were considering pulling out of Canada.

"Our local Hyundai dealer, concerned about the negative publicity, called a news conference and told reporters that he'd been assured the firm was not about to fold up. His comments were aired the same afternoon, on two radio stations and the local CBC outlet. The angle taken by all three was something to the effect that the local Hyundai dealer denies published reports in Toronto [that] the company is thinking of pulling out. He did a good job of getting his message across. His news conference was well organized, he had all the facts and figures ready to back up his points, and I think his customers were assured."

The only thing I would add to Vanderwoude's account is that you should also get the item corrected in the publications that initially got the story wrong.

John Campbell, News Director at Sudbury, Ontario-based Mid Canada Radio offered six possible remedies to an erroneous or misleading radio news broadcast:

1. Immediate retraction and correction using the program's announcer.
2. A retraction and correction in the next newscast that would use new information in "an equal or better profile" than in the original broadcast.
3. A retraction and correction broadcast the following day in the same "hour cast" as the original story in hopes of reaching the same audience that was misled.
4. An editorial in the complainant's own voice "(the radio version of a letter to the editor)...an option where there is a continuing disagreement, but no litigation contemplated."
5. A station-initiated apology.
6. An apology delivered by the station at the initiation of a complainant who has discussed the situation with the news director or station manager.

He added, "Several combinations of the above six points may be employed pending a conversation between the news director/station manager and the complainant."

And I will add that you should choose the remedy that will best enable you to get across the points you want to make to the publics you want to reach.

Unlike the print media, radio and television often give the subjects of a news story the opportunity to speak for themselves, without the intervention of reporters or editors to "cut and paste" interviews. Current affairs programming, much of it live or recorded and broadcast without editing, is becoming increasingly popular as radio and television attempt to bring major events and the people who make them happen right into our living rooms (or cars, as the case might be). And to enliven public debate, individuals, often taking opposite sides on key issues, are frequently pitted against each other in live interviews.

This puts a greater onus on the subject – on you – to correct inaccurate or misleading information on air as it occurs. As Mark

Starowicz, then Executive Producer of "The Journal," explained in response to my query about how the broadcast media handle corrections, "The nature of the program is such that corrections . . . generally are made on the spot, during the course of the program in interviews or discussions among guests. Unlike a newscast that reports events as a third party, 'The Journal' calls on participants themselves to describe, discuss or argue the topic or issue at hand; perceived errors or distortions are argued, if not resolved, during the broadcast. This is seen most clearly in the case of panel discussions but the same principle is followed in our documentaries: All parties involved are best heard by letting them do the talking themselves. 'The Journal's important obligation is to ensure that all sides are represented fairly."

Not all errors can be corrected by letting the guests do the talking themselves. Mr. Starowicz said that "on an occasion when a clear, unchallenged misstatement of fact of sufficient magnitude to justify a correction has been made in a program, we announce the error and correct it in a subsequent program. We have found that this is best done in the final minutes of a program. Small errors of detail are difficult to correct. We simply make a judgement."

Mr. Starowicz made another observation, this one of relevance to managers and executives who don't believe media training is necessary or to those reporters or editors who may disparage the media training process as an unwarranted attempt by managers and executives to learn how to avoid public disclosure.

"I note that in your seminar," he said in reference to a brochure describing my media relations course, "you make the important point that participants in interviews or discussions be able to express themselves clearly. One of our major tasks is obtaining guests with the credentials of expertise plus the ability to communicate that expertise so that 'The Journal' can meet the tests of fairness and balance in programming."

As I have said earlier, and as I will say again and again, to ensure accurate and comprehensive media coverage of your organization's activities and achievements, you have to learn how to communicate effectively with the media and through the media. And this holds true whether you are initiating a story, replying to a reporter's enquiry or attempting to correct an erroneous news item.

IN BRIEF

What to Do When the Media Get It Wrong

1. Get angry in private. Don't rant and rave to the reporter or editor.
2. Carefully analyze what was wrong with the story.
3. Call the reporter to discuss errors in the story and your proposed remedy:
    - Clarification or correction.
    - Letter to the editor.
    - Get new article published.
    - Write op-ed page article under your byline.
    - Complaint to the Press Council.
    - Legal action.
4. If the situation warrants, call the reporter's editor, but inform the reporter first.
5. Initiate your own media event by issuing a news release or calling a news conference.
6. Attack the story, not the reporter.

A System For 13
Learning From Your
Own Experience

Nobody is perfect – everybody makes mistakes. So chances are that sooner rather than later your news releases will be ignored, no one will come to your news conference, your interview will not be published, you'll squint into the camera, you'll make a damaging statement on the radio, or the Saturday feature will ignore your company's accomplishments, dwelling instead on its failures and exposing its warts.

Don't let these unavoidable experiences discourage you. As I said from the very beginning, managing the media does not give you complete control over the media. It merely increases the chances that your message will be reported in a positive way.

The converse is that with proper media relations you can reduce the chances of your positive story being ignored or of negative stories being published or broadcast. Viewed from this perspective, it's clear that some degree of failure is part of the job. It goes with your territory, just as Wayne Gretzky misses periodic shots on goal and Joe Carter has more strike-outs than home runs.

But this does not excuse you from the ongoing task of improving your rate of success. The first step in this process of self-improvement is frank and honest self-appraisal. It's not easy to admit that you made a mistake or failed in a particular mission, but that's what you've got to do. You don't have to shout your shortcomings from the rafters; just don't hide them from yourself, and don't look for scapegoats.

The story may have misquoted you, which may have been the reporter's fault. But don't stop there. Analyze what you said during the interview and how you could have been more concise and precise, thus reducing the likelihood that your words would either be misinterpreted or taken out of context.

Your news release didn't get the coverage that management wanted or you had hoped for. Perhaps the story itself lacked newsworthiness.

But look deeper. Could the lead in your news release have been punchier or pegged to a better news angle?

A few years ago, the Canadian Manufacturers' Association issued a public policy paper on the need to improve the effectiveness of government-sponsored research and development. The news release I wrote and distributed excited very little media interest. Recently, a similar policy document issued by the CMA received significant media coverage. The association's public affairs director pegged the news release on the number of Canadian jobs that could be lost if R&D efforts are not improved and he launched the paper at a Toronto news conference. You can learn from other people, too.

Monitoring Coverage

But first you have to distinguish between failure and success, figure out the cause of each, and apply the lessons you've learned to your next project.

So, after you've distributed your Media Information Kit, held your news conference and given your interviews, evaluate the quantity and the quality of the media coverage you received.

You do this by subscribing to a media clipping service and, if appropriate, a broadcast monitoring service. Bowdens is used most extensively, but you might want to try some of the specialized services listed in the Matthews directory. The clippings will tell you which publications used your story, how much of it they used and whether they based it on your news release, on interviews you may have given to a particular publication or on the story syndicated by Canadian Press or another wire service.

Study the clips, transcripts or tapes on a regular basis. Analyze what worked and what didn't. Ruthlessly evaluate how effective you were in getting your main points across in print and on the airwaves, and incorporate your ever-increasing knowledge and ever-finer judgement into successive media relations programs. In time, knowing the appropriate action to take in any given set of circumstances will become second nature to you.

Managing (the Media) by Objectives

Monitoring coverage may not be enough, however. Many media relations people remain under constant pressure to provide their employers or clients with some form of objective, quantifiable evaluation of their various media initiatives. To meet this need, I have developed an evaluation system called Managing (the Media) by Objectives.

The evaluation process has two distinct steps. The first is to measure the extent of the media coverage; the second to examine the nature of that coverage. Here's how it works:

Step One   As part of the planning process of your media initiative, establish targets of coverage. These may include specific publications or radio and TV stations that you want to pick up your story; the total amount of media coverage by number of media outlets; number of inches in type or minutes of air time, or a combination of both; the number of media enquiries or interviews that resulted from your initiative.

The combination of criteria you use would depend on the overall objectives of your program. If, for example, your company wants potential investors and stock analysts to know more about its strong financial performance during the past year, you would target the business media. The print media might include the *Globe and Mail's Report on Business*; the *Financial Post*; the *Financial Times*; *Macleans*; the business sections of the newspapers in such financial centres as Montreal, Toronto, Vancouver and, if you want to attract US investors, New York and Chicago as well. You could reach these publications directly, but to increase the chances that they will pick up your story, you might set a high priority on having your story carried by the major wire services – Canadian Press for the Canadian media, and the Reuters and Dow Jones wire services for the media in the United States and around the world.

And don't forget the broadcast media. Many radio and television stations air special business reports as part of their general news coverage and virtually all radio and television news broadcasts contain some business news. Decide whether your story is significant enough to earn mention on the business reports of the programs business people listen to or watch in the important cities and, if warranted, include these media on your list of criteria. Don't forget that all of these points, as well as some 75 Canadian brokerage houses, will be reached by Canada News-Wire and more than 200 by Canadian Corporate News.

Once you've decided on the coverage criteria, you must assign each criterion a value. You might, for example, regard coverage by local or network television as more important than coverage by local or network radio, but as less important than coverage in the business press. So rate them accordingly by assigning each criterion a point value, with the total equalling 10. Thus, the business press might have a value of four points, television coverage might be assigned a value of three points, local radio two points, with the remaining point assigned to coverage in other media.

Once the media initiative is over and you've studied the news clips and radio and television transcripts or tapes, you can determine the extent to which you achieved your targets.

Let's say the *Report on Business*, the *Toronto Star*, the *Montreal Gazette*, Canadian Press, the Dow Jones and Reuters all carried the story, but it was ignored by *Macleans* and the Vancouver media. That's very good coverage. You've hit a solid majority of your targeted media points. Out of a total of four points, I would give you a score of three.

Television coverage was not nearly as good. None of the networks carried the story, although it was picked up by two local Toronto stations. Score one out of three.

Radio fared a bit better, with the story carried by the CBC network. Score one out of two.

And newspapers in Halifax, Calgary and Edmonton published the story distributed by Canadian Press; so you pick up an added point.

This gives you a total of six points out of a possible 10 for Step One.

Step Two   Like Step One, this involves the setting of criteria and targets, but for Step Two they are intended to tell you not how much coverage you received, but rather the extent to which that coverage was good or bad, positive or negative, helpful or harmful.

The number of criteria may vary, depending on the objectives of the media initiative. It does seem logical, however, always to include the degree to which the key points of your news release were covered as one of your major criteria. Obviously, the more key points mentioned in the story and the degree to which those key points dominate the story, the better the story is from your perspective.

Step Two should also include what I call Positive-Negative Factor criteria. These criteria measure the attitudes the coverage will likely engender in the publics you are trying to reach. They might include mention in the media of past difficulties your organization had encountered; use of pejorative labels, such as "financially troubled," "debt-ridden," or "scandal-wracked"; other references that either enhance or detract from your organization's reputation (does the reporter quote respected individuals who dispute the key points of your story or use sarcasm and other literary devices to impugn your organization's integrity?); or the inclusion of damaging factual errors. In cases where past coverage of your organization has tended to include pejorative references, the mere omission of these may earn points for your media initiative.

Once you establish the various criteria, ascribe a value to each. As with Step One, the total maximum point value must equal 10. So let's say that the degree of coverage of your key points is worth half the battle and is assigned a value of five points, with the Negative-Positive Factor criteria getting the remaining five. Here too, you study the clips, transcripts and tapes of the media coverage you received and decide the degree to which you achieved the targets you set under the various criteria and how many points each separate criterion will be awarded.

But Step Two adds a wrinkle: The criteria falling under the Negative-Positive Factor can be awarded either positive or negative points, depending on the nature of the media coverage.

In our example, this means that the number of points awarded to this group of criteria can range from –5 to +5. The reason is simple – there must be a mechanism for measuring the damage that negative coverage can do to your organization. Oscar Wilde's quip that the only thing worse than being talked about is not being talked about may hold true in some circles. But I don't think it constitutes a universally valid approach to the practice of media relations.

Getting back to our example, assume you've studied all the clips and transcripts and discover that of your three key points, at least one was included in every one of the news accounts, with some of the financial publications mentioning two or all three. So you score four points out of a possible five.

Here's how the evaluation of the Negative-Positive Factor shapes up:

- Previous media coverage has tagged your organization with negative labels, so one of the goals of your current media initiative is to get the media to replace those pejorative labels with positive ones. Maximum value: Three points. While two of the news stories used the old labels, those stories along with most of the others also used the most upbeat quote contained in your news release. As a result, you score one point.

- Your company had a bitter strike several years ago during which it was convicted of unfair labour practices. You want to avoid reference to that incident in the current media initiative. Maximum value: One point. You win hands down on this one and get your point.

- You're aware that many other factors can affect the balance and tone of a story, so you assign the remaining point to cover these contingencies. Most of the news stories resulting from your media initiative confine themselves pretty much to the material in your media information kit and to the answers given to follow-up media enquiries. One of the major financial publications did, however, quote an unnamed financial analyst who disputed the validity of the major assertion in your news release. This will partially offset some of the other positive coverage you received, so you score −1 on this criterion.

This gives you five points in the Step Two evaluation. To arrive at your final rating, multiply the six points received in Step One by the five points received in Step Two, which gives a total score of 30.

Managing (the Media) by Objectives

Step One

Extent of coverage	Possible points	Actual points
Business and targeted publications	0 to 4	3
Television	0 to 3	1
Radio	0 to 2	1
Nontargeted publications	0 to 1	1
Total Step One points	0 to 10	6

Step Two

Nature of coverage	Possible points	Actual points
Key Points	0 to 5	4
Negative-Positive Factor Negative tags	−3 to 3	1
Previous labour problems	−1 to 1	1
General balance	−1 to 1	−1
Total Step Two points	−5 to 10	5

Total points

	Possible points	Actual points
(Step One x Step Two)	−50 to 100	30

You multiply the points from Step One by the points from Step Two in order to account for the full effect of any negative or positive values. The fact is, wide media coverage hurts you when that coverage is negative and helps you when that coverage is positive. If you get only limited media exposure, the effects of either positive or negative coverage will also be limited. Multiplying the Step One points by the Step Two points reflects these vitally important realities.

Let's say you earned only one point in Step One, but –5 points in Step Two. That would give a final evaluation score of –5 points, damaging to be sure, but on a pretty small scale. Now let's assume that you got fairly wide coverage, giving you, say, a total of 5 points, but that your Step Two points remained at –5. The total value of your media initiative would be –25. And that is a significant negative value, strongly indicating that your media initiative was a resounding failure.

If the point scores from Steps One and Two were added, as opposed to multiplied, the evaluations in these two examples would actually be reversed, with the less damaging media initiative scoring lower than the more damaging initiative (–4 points as against –5 points in the first example, and 0 points as against –25 points in the second example).

What do the numbers mean?

If a media program results in a negative rating, you are actually worse off now than before you undertook the initiative. A score hovering around zero indicates that your media initiative will have little effect, one way or the other, on your organization and, at best, was a waste of time. A score of 10 would indicate only marginal success, while 20 points would be good, and anything above 50 would be downright superb.

Up to now, Managing (the Media) by Objectives has been discussed in the context of media programs initiated by you, the media relations practitioner. The system can also be used to evaluate coverage in crisis situations or in other cases in which a story is initiated by the media, not by you. Just keep your expectations within reasonable limits. If you're laying off 30 per cent of your workforce or had to recall a defective product, a score of zero would be quite comforting. And bear in mind that during severe crises, when you're doing all you can to keep the various dikes plugged up, you may not have the time needed to design your evaluation form until after the story dies down.

Ideally, however, the decisions as to which criteria to include in the evaluation process and the weight to be given to each of them should be made during the planning stages of the media initiative. This forces you to identify those aspects of your story that will best help you achieve your organization's overall objectives and to target your publics and the media needed to reach them before you design your Media Information Kit, write your news release and distribute these materials to the media.

Doing this will not only give you the proper basis for evaluating your media initiative, it will also help ensure that the initiative itself will be successful.

Profiles   14
Of Some Successful
Media Initiatives

1. Building Public Support: The Amoco-Dome Merger

In April 1987, Amoco Canada announced its proposal to purchase Dome Petroleum. This sparked tremendous media interest and generated significant controversy, with several of Dome's key creditors and shareholders opposing the sale. In response, the deal was renegotiated to the satisfaction of the creditors, the overwhelming majority of shareholders and Investment Canada.

The controversy, however, was fuelled by three dissident shareholders who went to court in an unsuccessful attempt to block the sale. Amoco Canada, a wholly owned subsidiary of Amoco Corp. of Chicago, felt that ultimately the success of the merger would depend not only on the legality of the transaction, which seemed certain, but also on the degree to which the newly merged company would be accepted and supported by the Canadian public. This view stemmed partly from the fact that Investment Canada, whose approval was required by law, is a public agency accountable to the federal government and, by extension, to the people, and also partly by the fact that Amoco had pledged to sell 20 per cent of the company to Canadian investors in a series of public share offerings.

Public appreciation of the viability of the merged company and of the benefits it would bring to Canada would be essential if the company were to get full value for the shares it intended to sell.

This was the situation in January, 1988, when T. Don Stacy, Amoco Canada's President, was invited to address the weekly luncheon meeting of the Empire Club.

Objectives The primary objective of the speech was to garner widespread support for the Amoco-Dome merger by highlighting the contributions that Amoco Canada had made in the past to the economic well-being of Canada and by highlighting the financial soundness of the merger and the additional economic activity that would generate new jobs – not just in the oil patch, but all across the country – once the merger was completed.

Another prime objective was to help win acceptance of the terms of the merger among Dome's shareholders, who had not yet formally voted to approve the transaction. The speech was to give a clear signal to any who might have thoughts of renegotiating that the deal was the fairest possible and there would be no "sweetening of the pot."

Target Groups The primary targets were well-connected business and political figures, market and stock analysts, Dome shareholders, industry leaders and, to the extent that residual goodwill is essential to the success of any broadly based communications program, the general public as well. We were also mindful that employees of both companies, suppliers and customers would also be exposed to the media coverage given the speech, and we wished, as a byproduct of the event, to reassure these key publics that the merger would create a more secure and prosperous future for them.

Procedure The Empire Club was regarded as an ideal venue for three key reasons. First, those attending the luncheon meetings tend to be influential decision-makers. Second, the event would provide a convenient media platform, thus enhancing the opportunity for Mr. Stacy to reach a nationwide audience. Third, the prestigious nature of the Empire Club would enhance the standing and credibility of its luncheon speaker.

To help achieve these goals, we invited the media to attend the speech and a news conference immediately following. In addition, several key reporters were invited for private interviews with Mr. Stacy following the news conference.

We also created a Media Information Kit that contained the full text of the speech as well as the text of Mr. Stacy's opening remarks at the news conference, a news release highlighting the key points we wanted to make, a chronology of events relating to the purchase, and a biographical sketch and photograph of Mr. Stacy. The kit was distributed to reporters attending the luncheon or the news conference and was sent by courier to other reporters who could not attend. The news release was also distributed across the country by Canada

News-Wire in both French and English. Several days prior to the speech, a note to editors inviting reporters to attend the news conference was also distributed on Canada News-Wire.

The full text of Mr. Stacy's speech to the Empire Club follows along with the news release.

Notes for remarks
by T. Don Stacy
President
Amoco Canada Petroleum Company Ltd.

The Empire Club of Canada
Royal York Hotel
Toronto, Ontario
February 11, 1988

Thank you, (name of introducer), for your very kind introduction, and my thanks to the Empire Club for the invitation to address you here today.

Amoco Canada's offer to purchase Dome Petroleum is certainly getting its share of attention. During the last 10 months, I have learned what it's like to live under the glare of public scrutiny.

And that sits very well with us at Amoco. For, as Oscar Wilde once remarked, the only thing worse than being talked about is not being talked about.

There is, of course, a much more compelling reason to welcome the widespread media coverage and the extensive public debate about the proposed purchase.

The new merged company will play a major role in the future development of Canada's oil and natural gas resources. It will become one of Canada's leading employers. And it will contribute substantially to Canada's future industrial growth and economic prosperity.

Canadians have a right to know about the merger and what effect it will have on their well-being. And we, at Amoco Canada, welcome the opportunity to answer any questions that the public may ask.

The primary question is whether there is going to be a deal at all. We thought we had one last May, when both Amoco Canada and Dome worked out what each had regarded as a fair and equitable agreement. But some of Dome's lenders didn't agree, and we returned to the negotiating table for another round of hard bargaining.

Our task, as always, was to negotiate terms that would satisfy the needs and desires of a wide variety of sometimes disparate groups – banks, institutional investors, individual shareholders, the federal government, regulatory agencies, the management and employees of both companies and, of course, the general public.

In the end, we came up with a fair and generous package – one that will provide the greatest good to the greatest number. The $5.5 billion deal – the biggest in Canadian history – gives Dome's secured lenders an average of 95 cents on the dollar and its unsecured lenders an average of 45 cents on the dollar. Common shareholders are offered securities having a face value of approximately $1.47 per share and preferred shareholders $7.30 per share.

Of greater importance, the merger will guarantee the jobs and livelihoods of thousands of Dome employees. It will pump billions of dollars a year into the Canadian economy through wages, capital expenditures, taxes and royalties. It will ensure continued exploration and development of some of Canada's most promising natural resource properties. And it will bring the country closer to its goal of achieving a secure supply of energy.

So far, our acquisition of Dome has been approved by the federal government, by all of Dome's secured lenders and by a solid majority of Dome's unsecured lenders. Most common shareholders seem to endorse the deal. Only a small minority of preferred and common shareholders have challenged the classification and voting levels that were recommended by Amoco and subsequently approved by the Court of Queen's Bench of Alberta.

The recently concluded court proceedings have allowed us to proceed to the final stages of a lengthy and highly complex process.

We have dedicated a lot of energy toward the consummation of this deal and we have overcome several major hurdles. What remains now is the formal polling of creditors and shareholders and the final fairness hearing. We expect the final closing to occur by mid-year.

This acquisition is a mammoth undertaking for Amoco Canada, but it is one that the company eagerly accepts. From the merging of the two workforces to the implementation of enormous energy projects, the company will face unprecedented challenges in an industry already underscored by risk.

The stakes are always high in the chameleon-like and volatile oil patch. The energy industry harbours both uncertainty and dependability. It gives rise both to concern and optimism. It foments failure and despair, while it also engenders wealth and fulfillment.

In the past two years the price of oil dove from more than $30 a barrel to less than $10; then rose to above $20, only to come down once again in the face of OPEC's difficulty in controlling its own members' production rates.

But if the December meeting of the OPEC countries raised questions about the organization's effectiveness, it also reaffirmed the importance of oil to the economic well-being both of producing and of consuming countries.

Whichever way the winds of international discord may blow – however uncertain the present may seem to be – there is no doubt that the oil industry will be quick to adjust and adapt to any new events, and that, over the long haul, demand for oil and natural gas will remain strong.

Here in Canada signs of this brighter future are already visible.

The development of reserves in the Beaufort Sea and an increase in the number of enhanced oil recovery programs and heavy oil projects will likely proceed in the not-too-distant future.

These programs will, of course, be possible only through continued government cooperation. And so far, the policies of the present government have accomplished a great deal to temper the volatility of the oil industry.

The deregulation of the oil industry in 1985 and the subsequent deregulation of natural gas prices in 1986 have allowed petroleum companies to establish new markets for their products.

The 1985 action to phase out the Petroleum Revenue Tax has further encouraged investment to develop Canada's energy resources. And during the past two years, Canadian producers have doubled their drilling activity. By contrast, in the United States, which retains its Windfall Profits Tax, activity has risen by less than half the Canadian rate.

The proposed reduction in the general corporate tax rate to 28 per cent will undoubtedly have a positive impact on growth for all sectors of the Canadian economy. For the energy industry, it will certainly provide an incentive to increase investment in conventional oil and gas activities.

I also expect the recently negotiated free trade agreement with the United States to herald a new era of economic and industrial expansion in our two countries.

The prospect of unfettered access to the enormous market south of the border may seem awesome, at first glance, to many Canadian businesses. And to some, the challenge presented by an equal competition with Americans in our Canadian markets may seem a daunting undertaking.

But profits of doom are rarely vindicated, and we should give little credence to those who condemn free trade.

I feel I can speak on behalf of the Canadian oil industry when I say that free trade with the US will motivate investment in long-term projects requiring long-term markets. It will spur the creation of new jobs, raise our standard of living and give Canada increased economic strength and energy security.

Another milestone in the march toward future prosperity is the government's attack on Canada's oversized deficit. Our staggering national debt – proportionally larger than that of the United States – is the greatest single barrier to future economic security. It is the deadweight that can drown the hopes of a more prosperous life – not only for the working men and women of today, but for the generations that succeed them.

Ottawa's commitment to deficit reduction must rank, therefore, as one of the most significant contours on Canada's political horizon. As yesterday's budget confirmed, the deficit can be managed.

But bringing the national deficit below the $30 billion level is not the final objective. It is merely a vantage point from which we can look upon further reductions in the months and years ahead. The long and gruelling process of deficit reduction has only just begun, and it is up to all of us to ensure that the government has the necessary support to see it through.

For its part, Amoco Canada is confident about the future of the Canadian economy and of the long-term viability of the nation's oil and gas sector. And we at Amoco are committed today, as we have been for the past 40 years, to the beneficial development of Canada's energy resources.

From our modest beginnings in 1948, when we operated out of rooms in Calgary's Palliser Hotel, we have grown into one of the most significant oil and gas developers in Canada.

During the past four decades, we have drilled more than 3,300 wells and added one billion barrels of oil and six trillion cubic feet of natural gas to Canada's reserves.

We spend almost $500 million annually on capital projects and operating activities in Canada. More than 22,000 people across the country owe their jobs directly or indirectly to these ongoing programs.

Amoco Canada has paid over $4.5 billion in direct taxes to government during the past 10 years. And every year, Amoco Canada contributes approximately $1.8 billion to the country's Gross Domestic Product, $3.6 billion to the gross output of Canadian industry and more than $600 million to the incomes of Canadian households.

These contributions will not only continue once the Dome purchase is complete, but they will grow, and grow substantially. The merged company will become the largest petroleum production enterprise in Canada, with a truly impressive pool of financial, technological and human resources.

Amoco's agreement with Investment Canada demonstrates our continued commitment to this country. The agreement, reached after rigorous negotiating, is one in which both parties can be justifiably proud.

To ensure that the mind and spirit of the new company remain in Canada, Amoco has agreed to enlarge its Board of Directors from nine to at least 12 members, at least two-thirds of whom will be Canadians and half of whom will be outside directors. We will continue to have Canadians in at least 70 percent of our executive management positions and we will offer employment to virtually all of Dome's employees.

We will allocate at least $2.5 billion over the next five years to exploration, development, pipeline construction and other capital projects. This is about $1 billion more than would have been spent separately by Amoco and Dome.

Our capital projects will stimulate growth in a variety of industries across the country, with a particular boost to the manufacturing and service sectors. Of the thousands of new jobs that will be created by Amoco's enhanced capital program, it is expected that more than 30 per cent will be in Central and Atlantic Canada.

The ongoing discovery and refinement of improved technology is critical to the successful development of oil sands, the Beaufort Sea reserves, heavy oil deposits and enhanced oil recovery programs. Towards this end, Amoco has earmarked $100 million to be spent in Canada over the next five years for experimental and applied research.

And, as part of our commitment to Canada, 20 per cent of Amoco Canada's voting stock will be made available to Canadian investors in a series of public offerings that will begin within five years after the acquisition of Dome is completed.

I have bombarded you with a lot of gee-whiz numbers today – a billion dollars for this, another three billion for that.

My motive, in part, was to impress you with the sheer magnitude of our activities and of our considerable contribution to the wealth and prosperity of Canada.

It was an expression of my desire to gain your understanding and your support for Amoco Canada and for what we are doing.

We do recognize, after all, that Canadians from all walks of life and from all regions of the country are essential to our corporate well-being.

Unless Canadians realize that the oil and gas sector as a whole and that Amoco in particular provide significant benefits to this country, we would not get approvals for our activities and we would not participate in the development of critical public policy affecting our industry.

Without the ever-present support of our workforce, Amoco would lack the skill, creativity, innovation and dedication needed to remain vital and competitive.

And without the backing of investors, Amoco would lack the capital needed to expand our operating base and develop the natural resources upon which our corporate livelihood depends.

What it comes down to is this: I believe in the future of Canada and in the positive contribution that Amoco Canada will make.

Canada is a young nation, full of strength and vigour.

It is blessed with bountiful mineral resources, landscapes of unmatched natural beauty and a population enriched by a mosaic of cultural and ethnic backgrounds.

But Canada, at times, still seems uncertain of its full potential. It is still refining its particular sense of nationhood and its proper role within the family of nations.

The decisions and actions we take today as business people will contribute mightily to this continuing process of nation-building, with the consequences reaching far beyond the fate of a single company or a single industry.

Amoco's acquisition of Dome and the success or failure of the merged company will affect more than its 5,500 employees, more than the wealth of those who will hold equity in the company and more than the people who rely upon its products.

The acquisition will play a part in determining whether Canada's energy industry grows or stagnates. And this, surely, will have a significant impact on Canada's drive for economic prosperity and energy self-sufficiency.

FOR IMMEDIATE RELEASE

TORONTO, February 11, 1988 – The soon-to-be merged Amoco Canada Petroleum Company Ltd. and Dome Petroleum Limited "will pump billions of dollars a year into the Canadian economy" and help the country become self-sufficient in energy, T. Don Stacy, Amoco Canada's President, said today.

Mr. Stacy told a luncheon meeting of the Empire Club of Canada that the merger will "ensure continued exploration and development of some of Canada's most promising natural resource properties, and it will bring the country closer to its goal of achieving a secure supply of energy."

He said the merged company "will allocate at least $2.5 billion over the next five years for exploration, development, pipeline construction and other capital projects. This is $1 billion more than would have been spent separately by Amoco and Dome."

He said Amoco has additionally earmarked $100 million to be spent in Canada over the next five years for experimental and applied research, which is critical to "the successful development of the oil sands, the Beaufort Sea reserves, heavy oil deposits and enhanced oil recovery programs."

These activities "will stimulate growth in a variety of industries across the country" and create "thousands of new jobs."

He said he expects the closing of the $5.5 billion acquisition to take place by mid-year.

"What remains now is the formal polling of creditors and shareholders and the final fairness hearing," which will enable the court "to ensure that all parties have been dealt with appropriately."

Mr. Stacy said the new merged company will "contribute substantially to Canada's future industrial growth and economic prosperity."

During the past 10 years, Amoco Canada has paid more than $4.5 billion in direct taxes, and every year contributes about $1.8 billion to Canada's gross domestic product, $3.6 billion to the gross output of Canadian industry and more than $600 million to the incomes of Canadian households.

"These contributions will not only continue once the Dome purchase is complete, but they will grow, and grow substantially," he said.

And "to ensure that the mind and spirit of the new company remain in Canada," Amoco Canada's Board of Directors will be enlarged and its Canadian content increased, and at least 70 per cent of its executive management positions will be occupied by Canadians.

Mr. Stacy said Canadian ownership in the petroleum industry will be increased, with 20 per cent of Amoco Canada's voting stock "made available to Canadian investors in a series of public offerings that will begin within five years after the acquisition of Dome is complete."

"I believe in the future of Canada and in the positive contribution that Amoco Canada will make," he said.

-30-

Contact: Dick Brown (416) 496-2243

Comment In evaluating the effectiveness of the event, the primary criterion was the extent and the nature of the media coverage of Mr. Stacy's remarks, either in the speech or in the news conference and interviews that followed.

We did quite well. The event received extensive print and broadcast media coverage, with reporters drawing on the Media Information Kit as well as the news conference and private interviews. There were reports in all major Canadian dailies and business publications. The speech, in its entirety, was broadcast over cable channels in Metro Toronto, and excerpts of the speech and news conference were transmitted by News Radio and Broadcast News and aired by radio stations across the country. In addition, the speech generated radio interviews with company spokespersons, who had yet another chance to stress the benefits the merger would bring to the Canadian economy.

As to be expected, the print coverage relied less on the speech than on the news conference or individual interviews that followed.

Most reporters would rather craft a story based on a lively exchange of dialogue than on words spoken from a prepared text. One reason is that words spoken off the cuff seem to have more credibility than written texts. I'm not sure that's really valid; many people (though, happily in this case, not Mr. Stacy) get nervous when speaking extemporaneously, especially in such nerve-wracking situations as news conferences and interviews, and thus may actually say things that are wrong or so disjointed that they will be easily misconstrued.

On the other hand, written texts are more carefully constructed, are reviewed and edited repeatedly and therefore, one may argue, more accurately reflect the meaning and intentions of the speaker than impromptu remarks.

There are other reasons for the media's preference for face-to-face interviews over prepared texts. A written text is clearly an expression of the speaker's agenda; responses to direct questions either at a news conference or one-on-one interview fit more with the reporter's agenda. Many reporters, if they have the time and energy, would rather follow their own agenda, because they believe this will enable them to make an independent judgement (or justify a prejudice, as the case might be). Also, a prepared text is confining; it is communication down a one-way street. Dialogue allows traffic to move in both directions and opens up further areas to explore and write about, giving good reporters a better opportunity to add special nuance or flavour to their coverage.

This is clearly reflected in the coverage given to Mr. Stacy's speech and subsequent news conference. But, through effective preparation and execution, you can greatly increase the likelihood that, no matter how the various reporters attack the subject and no matter how varied their coverage may be, you will convey your essential message and engender positive perceptions.

That Mr. Stacy succeeded is reflected in the coverage he received. The headline in the *Toronto Sun* proclaimed "22,000 new jobs forecast in deal."

The *Star* reported that Mr. Stacy "said the merged Dome-Amoco will play a major role in the development of Canada's energy resources. The company will be the largest natural gas producer and the second-largest Canadian oil producer."

It added that Mr. Stacy "said Amoco will spend at least $2.5 billion on exploration and development in the next five years, which is $1 billion more than both would have spent separately. That will lead to thousands of new jobs in the manufacturing and service sectors, roughly one-third of which will end up in central Canada."

The *Star* article – headlined "Preferred shareholders won't get a dime more says Amoco" – hammered this vital point home, quoting Mr. Stacy as saying "that his company's $5.5 billion offer for Dome is fair and equitable and while the shareholders have every right to appeal, the terms of the largest deal in Canadian business history won't be changed.

" 'Adding more money is absolutely out of the question,' Stacy told reporters following a luncheon speech delivered yesterday to the Empire Club."

The *Globe and Mail* article followed a similar tack. Under the headline "Amoco says its Dome bid isn't going to get any sweeter," reporter Kimberley Noble wrote that "Amoco's $5.5 billion bid for troubled Dome Petroleum Ltd. is as sweet as it's going to get, the president of Amoco Canada Petroleum Co. Ltd. says."

After outlining the terms of the deal, the article noted that "the new company, which will have about $8 billion in assets and $4 billion in debt, will embark on a five-year program aimed at rationalizing operations and personnel, divesting itself of assets and investments, cutting its debt and starting to sell equity back to the Canadian public."

And, like virtually all of the media accounts of the speech and news conference, the *Globe* reported that "the company has also slated $2.5 billion for exploration over the next five years, $1 billion more than was to be spent by the two independent companies."

The *Calgary Sun*'s article said "in a speech to Toronto's blue-chip Empire Club of Canada, Stacy described the $5.5 billion deal as 'fair and generous.'

"But he admitted Amoco can't get the deal through all its approvals 'unless Canadians realize that the oil and gas sector – and Amoco in particular – provides significant benefits to this country.'

"The acquisition . . . 'will play a part in determining whether Canada's energy industry grows.' "

The underlying goal of any media relations program is to instil positive attitudes among key publics, so that these people will respond in favourable ways as situations arise in the immediate, intermediate and distant future.

Amoco needed understanding of and support for the merger among many groups, and the perceptions generated by the speech would undoubtedly manifest themselves in the critical weeks and months that followed, as the proposed merger would be tested in the courts, voted on by shareholders, approved by lenders and evaluated by employees and the general public.

The sustained positive effect of the speech, of the media coverage that followed it and, indeed, of the overall public relations and communications program, was most clearly evident in the lead editorial of the September 1, 1988, edition of the *Globe and Mail*, which enthusiastically endorsed the merger.

The editorial said:

The absorption of Dome

Many interests will benefit today when Amoco Canada Petroleum Co. Ltd. completes the largest corporate takeover in Canadian history by digesting Dome Petroleum Ltd. of Calgary for $5.5 billion. This outcome is good for the West and clearly in the national interest.

It rescues Dome from bankruptcy, which greatly reduces the pain that most stakeholders would have felt in the worst-case scenario. Alberta and the petroleum industry will be spared an even more destructive loss of jobs and activity in the oil patch. Four major Canadian banks will recover 95 per cent of the approximately $2.3 billion they are owed, and unsecured creditors will receive 45 cents on the dollar. Even Dome's preferred and common shareholders will get something instead of nothing for their equity (though some still feel poorly treated).

Fortunately, Dome is worth more than the sum of its parts in the context of Amoco's Canadian operations.

Amoco Canada is a wholly owned subsidiary of Amoco Corp. of Chicago. But Dome is not a Canadian-controlled company either (though it has many Canadian shareholders). In any case, Amoco's bid was the best of three for Dome.

Two other bidders, Imperial Oil Ltd. and Canadian-controlled TransCanada PipeLines Ltd., lost out for Dome in the spring of 1987. Subsequent court challenges revealed that the bidding process was fair and the outcome just. Moreover, Amoco has made several attractive commitments to Investment Canada:

- There will be no further layoffs at Dome Petroleum.
- The new company, Amoco Dome, will spend $2.5 billion on resource development within the next five years – about $1 billion more than the companies had planned to spend separately (assuming world oil prices do not collapse).
- No dividends will be paid to Amoco Corp. for five years.
- Within 15 years, 20 per cent of Amoco Dome will be sold in a public share offering, the first time Amoco Corp. has accepted public participation in a subsidiary.

Most important, work can proceed aggressively on Dome's extensive oil and gas leases, which have been under-developed in the shadow of bankruptcy. Amoco plans to sell some of Dome's assets, but the new company will emerge as one of the strongest on the production side of the industry. This will be good for employment and, in the long run, for Canada's energy security.

2. Rebuilding an Image: The Case of Quintette Coal

Quintette Coal Limited, which has a major coal mining and processing operation in northeastern British Columbia, had borne the brunt of critical media coverage for years, in part because of start-up problems and in part because of unforeseen weaknesses in coal markets.

As a result, the operation did not live up to the potential that was forecast when the decision to proceed with production was made in the early 1980s. At that time, the lenders, the project partners, the federal and BC governments (which provided essential transportation and port facilities) and independent analysts all projected rising prices and demand for coal, projections which failed to materialize.

Meanwhile, the operators of the mine and processing plants were steadily ironing out the problems, increasing production and productivity and reducing unit costs. These achievements greatly improved the company's earnings situation, despite the continuing weakness of world coal prices. As far as the company was concerned, the long-term outlook for Quintette was growing brighter every month. Unfortunately, negative perceptions about the company persisted, particularly among the British Columbia media.

To rectify the situation, the company wanted to publicize significant accomplishments. To build its credibility with both the media and the investment community, the decision was made to present those accomplishments in a balanced way. The outcome was the following news release, which speaks not only of a "significant milestone" reached by the company, but also of the need to restructure debt because of "soft markets and weak prices for coal."

FOR IMMEDIATE RELEASE

Quintette reaches production milestone

VANCOUVER, July 29, 1986 – Quintette Coal Limited has reached a "significant milestone" by meeting or exceeding the production and cash-flow targets set when the project was being developed in the early 1980s, company President Paul Kostuik said today.

During the second quarter of 1986, Quintette produced clean coal at its annual design rate of 6.3 million tonnes. At the same time, cash production costs were lower and the cash margin higher during the 90-day period than required under the full completion criteria established in the credit agreement with the project's lenders.

In addition, the 1,000 kilometre rail link operated by BC Rail Limited and Canadian National Railway between the mine and the coal terminal at Prince Rupert and the new port facilities operated by Ridley Island Terminal proved their ability to handle design-rate production from Quintette.

"These achievements reflect the dedication of our workforce, and they firmly demonstrate the strong underlying potential of Quintette, in which shareholders, financial institutions and governments have invested," Mr. Kostuik said.

"We can now face the future with the knowledge that, from a production standpoint, Quintette is a viable operation. We can produce at our design rate, and we can do it at or below the unit costs projected when the mine was being planned," he said.

For the present, however, Mr. Kostuik said "soft markets and weak prices for coal are forcing Quintette to limit production during the remainder of 1986. Until markets improve, we will operate at a rate of about 5 million tonnes per year and, accordingly, we expect unit costs per tonne will rise."

"As a result of this, ongoing cash flow will be more severely restricted and the Company is obliged to seek restructuring of its debt, and discussions with the lenders are taking place."

-30-

Contact: Paul Kostuik (604) 669-2226, or
Ed Shiller (416) 865-1991 or (416) 496-2243

The release, which was distributed on the business, mining and oil networks of Canada News-Wire, had the desired results, as the following article in the Vancouver Province of July 29, 1986, illustrates:

Coal hits stride
by Patrick Durrant, Business Reporter

Quintette Coal Ltd. has finally reached the production and cash flow targets set when its northeastern B.C. coal project was being developed in the early 1980s.

Company president Paul Kostuik said yesterday Quintette produced clean coal at its annual design rate of 6.3 million tonnes during the quarter ended June 30.

At the same time, production costs were lower and the cash margin higher during the quarter than required under the full-completion criteria established in the credit agreement with Quintette's bankers.

However, the production achievement was short-lived. Kostuik said the weak market for coal is forcing the company to limit production during the remainder of 1986.

Until markets improve, the mine will operate at a rate of about five million tonnes a year and unit costs are expected to rise above the levels achieved during the second quarter.

"As a result, cash flow will be more severely restricted, obliging the company to seek early restructuring of its debt." Kostuik said. "Discussions with the lenders are taking place."

Quintette plans to make the first scheduled principal repayment on its debt on July 31.

But repayment over the original period of the loan is "improbable" in light of current and expected near-term market conditions for thermal and metallurgical coal.

A revised development plan recently presented to the company's lenders includes estimated mid-term savings of $235 million in capital and production costs, as compared with the prior plan presented early in 1985.

Quintette's parent, Denison Mines Ltd., has hired an independent consultant (former Canadair president Gil Bennett) to recommend a restructuring plan and to assist in implementing it.

Commenting on Quintette's second-quarter performance, Kostuik said: "We can now face the future with the knowledge that, from a production standpoint, Quintette is a viable operation. We can produce at our design rate, and we can do it at the unit costs projected when the mine was being planned."

It's clear that the reporter did his homework by gathering additional information about the revised development plan and the debt restructuring. But overall, the story closely mirrors the news release; indeed, all the quotes used by the reporter were taken from the release.

By carefully identifying the key points it wanted to make, by including quotable quotes from the president that incorporated those points and by adhering to proper journalistic style and content, the company gave the reporter usable information in a usable form. And by thus meeting the needs of the media, the news release increased the chances that the company's message would be reported in a balanced and accurate way.

3. Debating Public Policy: CMA's Response to a Speech from the Throne

Like any major public policy group, the Canadian Manufacturers' Association wants to be quoted on its reaction to significant political or economic developments. So it was natural that, as the CMA's public relations consultant, I would prepare and distribute a news release on a recent Throne Speech. It serves as a good illustration of the kinds of decisions that must be made when dealing with even the most straightforward of events.

The writing of the news release followed an established routine. There were several issues vital to manufacturers that the CMA either expected or wanted to be raised in the Throne Speech – reducing the federal deficit, enhancing international trade, developing a national science policy and implementing favourable tax reform, among others. I listened to the Throne Speech, keeping a kind of scorecard comparing how the government and the CMA regarded certain issues. The content and tone of the release followed from that.

Objectives   The CMA's aim in all of this was threefold.

First, it wanted to let the government know publicly where it stood on the issues; what it would support and what it would oppose. The emphasis here is on "publicly." You've got to put your money where your mouth is. Many business groups lost credibility with the Mulroney government following the 1985 budget, when they failed to support a budget provision that would have ended the indexing of Canada pensions. These groups heavily lobbied the government to reduce the deficit, pledging to support whatever measures the government proposed. In the end, though, most of these business lobbies opposed the pension reform. Mulroney went out on a limb, and almost ended up falling out of the tree.

Second, it wanted to increase the public's awareness of the issues as part of the process of moulding public opinion.

Third, it wanted to demonstrate to the CMA's members and potential members that the CMA was an effective organization to which they should belong.

Strategy The timing and intensity of the news event – a mid-afternoon Throne Speech that would constitute a very busy one-day story – and the CMA's objective of reaching as wide an audience as possible, dictated:

1. That we tell our story immediately. Even waiting until the next day would have sharply limited the chances of our views being reported in the media's reaction stories;
2. That we keep our message short and simple; and
3. That we distribute our message to as wide a range of media as possible.

Procedure My course of action was pretty clear. My Media Information Kit would consist of nothing more than a one-page news release, which I would distribute on Canada News-Wire's Canadian Business and Financial Network. As a further refinement, I asked that the release be directed to "News Editors" and not, as is usual practice with stories sent on the Network, to "Business Editors."

The reason was that I wanted the story to go to the business publications that are not on Canada News-Wire's Basic Network. But the story was not primarily a business story, it was a national political story. As such, I figured it would be handled by the news desk. I didn't want my release getting lost in the shuffle between departments.

The Throne Speech coincided with an internal CMA meeting that would keep all the senior people incommunicado all day, so there was reason to make prior arrangements for media interviews. It was agreed that I would handle whatever came along if I couldn't get hold of the president, who would be at the meeting. As a crib sheet, I would use the news release that I was to write.

To make the correct decisions about the nature of the media opportunity, the nature of the media material I was going to prepare and my method of distribution, I had to follow the critical path outlined in Chapter 2, a process that should be followed in developing a media approach to even such a routine event as the Throne Speech. In an ideal world, every significant development that takes place within your organization or can have an impact on the well-being of your organization should be subjected to this type of analysis.

Here is the text of the news release:

FOR IMMEDIATE RELEASE
Throne Speech sets positive agenda, CMA President says

TORONTO, October 1, 1986 – "Today's Throne Speech, though general in nature, indicates that the federal government has a grasp of the challenges facing our economy and represents a positive agenda for action," Laurent Thibault, President of The Canadian Manufacturers' Association, said.

"Restoring sound fiscal management by reducing the national debt, continuihg to cut the deficit, ensuring a decline in the government's financial requirements and pursuing effective expenditure restraint are essential priorities for a healthy economy, and are among the most important commitments contained in the Throne Speech," Mr. Thibault said.

"Other positive aspects were recognition of the important role that international trade will play in the well-being of Canada and of the need to improve our international competitiveness," he said.

"The government's commitment to negotiating a mutually beneficial bilateral trade agreement with the United States, to pursuing multilateral trade talks under the auspices of the General Agreement on Tariffs and Trade and to developing new trade opportunities with Japan and other Pacific Rim countries should benefit all of Canada," he said.

"A key factor in Canada's success as an industrial and trading nation will be our ability to develop and implement new technologies, and the range of initiatives to stimulate technological development outlined in the Throne Speech is a critical step towards that goal," Mr. Thibault said.

Mr. Thibault said "the CMA supports the government's pledge to simplify the country's corporate tax structure. We hope, however, that the promise of reform will include abolition of the highly unfair manufacturer's sales tax and assurance that our tax system will be competitive and attract investment."

-30-

Contact: Ed Shiller (416) 496-2243

The strategy paid off. The CMA president was one of only three non-government people to be quoted for reaction in the *Toronto Star*, with his remarks taken verbatim from the news release. And I, using the news release as a guide, was interviewed by Broadcast News and Radio Canada.

4. Celebrating an Event: The Blessing of the Bells

The construction of the Slovak Cathedral of the Transfiguration was a natural draw for the media from the moment the cornerstone was laid in 1984. The structure itself is imposing, rising more than 200 feet and dominating the gently rolling agricultural landscape of Markham, Ontario, just outside Toronto.

Pope John Paul consecrated the cathedral during his visit to Canada in September 1984, marking the first time a Roman Pontiff had blessed a church in North America. Nearly two years later, the bells that would sit in the three towers were due to arrive from the foundry in France.

The occasion was one of celebration for Canada's 30,000 Slovak Catholics, and many of them planned to be at the cathedral when the bells were hoisted into position on July 7, 1986. It would be a natural media event, and the Eparchy (Diocese) hoped the ensuing news and feature coverage would inform the general public of the presence of the cathedral and tell something of the background of the Byzantine Rite, to which many Slovak Catholics belong.

Procedure   The news peg was the size of the bells (the world's largest peal), which was the natural lead of the news release. But to the Slovak community, the real story was, to quote the bishop, the "magnificent building from which to spread the Good News spoken by Christ and to which we can call the people to worship." So this, too, was put into the news release.

But there was much more to tell – details of the casting of the bells and their journey to Canada, the story behind the naming of the bells and descriptions of the carvings and inscriptions that adorn them, a detailed description of the cathedral and historical information about the Slovak Byzantine Rite. This was much too much information to include in a single release. If we had tried, the document would have been so filled with detail that the main points we wanted to get across might have been missed by the media.

So we kept the news release relatively short, giving only the skeleton of the story, which was fleshed out just a bit with a key quote from the bishop. The other information, which we felt some reporters might want to use for feature articles, was contained in clearly marked fact sheets.

The media kits – containing the news release, fact sheets, a 5" by 7" photo of the bells and a covering letter describing the upcoming event – were sent by courier to all media in Metro Toronto and nearby communities four days before the event. This enabled the media, particularly the TV stations, to evaluate the newsworthiness of the event, to plan their coverage and to assign crews.

Just about every radio and TV station and newspaper between Toronto and Barrie carried the story, with virtually all reports conveying the message the Eparchy wanted to get across. Some reporters relied primarily on the news release, others conducted interviews at the site with church officials and community people. All used information contained in the fact sheets.

The Media Kit   Following are the written materials contained in the Media Information Kits:

July 3, 1986

Note to Editors and Reporters,

The three bells forming the largest peal of bells in the world will arrive at the Slovak Cathedral of the Transfiguration in Markham on Monday, July 7, 1986, at 10 A.M.

They will be lifted by crane from the transport and hoisted, one by one, into the 210-foot-high centre tower of the cathedral, situated on the west side of Woodbine Avenue, just north of Major Mackenzie Boulevard.

There will be no formal ceremony to mark this occasion, although Bishop Michael Rusnak, Eparch of Canada's 30,000 Slovak Byzantine Catholics, will be present. Mr. Paccard of Paccard S.A., the French foundry that cast the bells, will also be at the site. The media are invited to cover the arrival of the bells, and I am enclosing a news release and background information.

In a formal ceremony on August 10, Cardinal Carter will bless the bells, which will then be rung publicly for the first time.

If you have any questions, please call me at (416) 496-2243.

Yours sincerely,
Ed Shiller

FOR IMMEDIATE RELEASE

World's largest peal of bells arrives at Markham cathedral

MARKHAM, Ontario, July 7, 1986 – The world's largest peal of bells arrived at their new home today, the Slovak Cathedral of the Transfiguration, following a 28-day, 4,000-mile land and sea journey from a foundry in France.

The three bells – weighing 37,000 pounds, 21,000 pounds and 13,000 pounds – were lifted by crane from the truck that drove them from the port of Halifax and hoisted into their permanent home in the 210-foot-high centre tower of the as-yet-unfinished cathedral.

The cathedral and its cornerstone were blessed by Pope John Paul II during his visit to Canada in September 1984. This marked the first time that a Roman Pontiff consecrated a church in North America.

Cardinal Carter, Archbishop of Toronto, will bless the bells, and they will be rung for the first time, at a public ceremony on Sunday, August 10, 1986. They will be christened St. Stephen, St. Anne and the Prophet Daniel. A carving on each bell depicts a scene from the life of its namesake. St. Stephen, the largest of the three and the 13th largest single bell in the world, is dedicated to Pope John Paul.

The three bells were cast in bronze at the foundry of Paccard S.A. in the French town of Annecy. St. Stephen is virtually the same size as the bell in the Basilique du Sacré Coeur in Paris, which the Paccard foundry cast in 1898.

The Cathedral of the Transfiguration is the cathedral for the Eparchy (Diocese) of Sts. Cyril and Methodius. The Eparchy was established by Pope John Paul in 1980 to serve Canada's 30,000 Slovak Catholics who are part of the Byzantine Rite. The faithful of the Byzantine Rite form the second largest group in the Catholic Church after the Latin, or Roman, Rite.

"With the arrival of the bells and the Cathedral itself nearing completion, we have a magnificent building from which to spread the Good News spoken by Christ and to which we can call the people to worship," Bishop Michael Rusnak, the Eparch of Canada's Slovak Byzantine Catholics, said today.

-30-

Contact: Ed Shiller (416) 496-2243

Fact Sheet:

The Bells for the Cathedral of the Holy Transfiguration

Size:

St. Stephen - 37,000 pounds.

St. Anne - 21,000 pounds.

Prophet Daniel - 13,000 pounds.

Together they form the largest peal of bells in the world, weighing 71,000 pounds. St. Stephen, the world's 13th largest bell, is virtually the same size as the bell, named Savoyarde, in the Basilique du Sacré Coeur in Paris. The Sacré Coeur bell is slightly heavier by virtue of a crown placed around its top.

Casting:

By Paccard S.A. in Annecy, France, one of Europe's oldest and most respected foundries. The bells are cast in bronze, consisting of 80 per cent copper and 20 per cent Malaysian tin.

Transportation and Hoisting:

The bells were carried by truck from the foundry in Annecy, France, to Le Havre; shipped to Halifax on the Atlantic Service, a container ship belonging to ACL Canada Inc.; and trucked from Halifax to Markham by K.C. Transportation Services Incorporated of Nova Scotia. The journey, beginning on June 9, took 28 days.

Perwin Construction Company Limited is the general contractor for the cathedral, and Nadrofsky Corporation is the hoisting contractor for the bells.

The hoisting of the bells – by a 400-tonne crane – will take about four hours and will begin shortly after they arrive at the cathedral at 10 A.M. on Monday, July 7.

Naming of the Bells:
Bells are one of the liturgical signs of the Church that remind the people of the Good News spoken by Christ and call them to worship. Church bells are always blessed and named after one of the saints.

The bells will be blessed by His Eminence, Cardinal Carter, Archbishop of Toronto, in a public ceremony beginning at 2 P.M. on Sunday, August 10, 1986. They will be christened St. Stephen, St. Anne and the Prophet Daniel. From high in their position in the cathedral's centre tower, the bells will then be rung publicly for the first time. A mass of the Byzantine Rite will then be celebrated.

St. Stephen is named after the first martyr for Christ who was killed by stoning around the year 37 A.D. His story is related in the Acts of the Apostles. The carving on the bell depicts St. Stephen being stoned and lifting up his hands to God. Inscribed below the carving are his words before death: "Behold, I see the heavens opened and the Son of man standing at the right hand of God" (Acts 7:56).

This bell is dedicated to Pope John Paul II, whose figure is carved on the side opposite St. Stephen's. The text of a telegram the Pope delivered to the cathedral for the celebration in honour of St. Methodius on July 7, 1985, is also inscribed on the bell. It reads:

On the occasion of the 1,100th anniversary of the death of St. Methodius, which you are celebrating together at the Cathedral with the Holy Liturgy, I assure you that I am with you in spirit. On this auspicious occasion, I am sending you my warm greetings and bestowing upon you my apostolic blessing.

The bell is dated the same year as the Pope's message. Below it are inscribed the words: "Preserve, O

Lord, the fullness of Thy Church" from the Divine Liturgy of St. John Chrysostom. This is the Liturgy celebrated by Christians of the Byzantine Rite.

Next to the Pope are carvings of the holy brothers Sts. Cyril and Methodius, who were responsible for the Christianization of the Slovaks and the Slavs. Below is an inscription taken from St. Cyril's prayer before death: "Let Thy Church increase into a multitude, gather all into a union of spirit and form of them an excellent people."

St. Anne is named for the mother of Mary the Mother of God. As the grandmother of Christ, St. Anne is intermediary between the Old and New Testaments and forerunner of the Good News. Devotion to St. Anne became widespread in the East by the 4th century. One of her best known shrines is St. Anne de Beaupré in Quebec. She is a model for all women in the married state and charged with the rearing of children. The carving on the bell depicts St. Anne with her child Mary. Inscribed below are the words: "He has helped his servant Israel in remembrance of his mercy" (Luke 1:54) taken from the Magnificat of Mary.

Daniel is named after the celebrated prophet of the Book of Daniel in the Old Testament. Daniel was one of the young men of the tribe of Judah taken in captivity from Jerusalem to Babylon in 605 B.C. and chosen to serve there in the pagan king's palace. Resisting all pressures to worship false gods, Daniel steadfastly maintained his faith in the one God at all costs. When he continued to worship God against an ordinance of King Darius, he was cast into a den of lions. His faith preserved him and the Lord delivered him from danger. The carving on the bell depicts Daniel surrounded by the lions as he prays fervently to God. Inscribed below the carving are the words taken from the Book of Daniel: "The people who know their God shall stand firm and take action" (Daniel 11:32).

Background Information:

The Cathedral of the Transfiguration

The cathedral, in the Township of Markham, about 25 kilometres north of Toronto, is named in honour of the Transfiguration of Our Lord and Saviour Jesus Christ. The Lord Jesus revealed His glory to the three chosen disciples, Peter, James and John, on the holy mountain Tabor. Appropriately built on a rise of land, the cathedral will stand as a splendid symbol of this awesome mystery.

The three front towers represent the three persons of God as well as the Mystery of the Transfiguration itself. When Peter beheld the transfigured Christ, he exclaimed: "Lord, it is good for us to be here. If thou wilt, let us set up three tents here, one for thee, one for Moses, and one for Elias" (Matthew 17:4).

The centre tower, named the Tower of the Transfiguration, stands 210 feet high and will contain a triumphant peal of bells cast in France and christened St. Stephen, St. Anne and the Prophet Daniel. On the front side of the tower above the main door, will be a semicircular mosaic of Mary, the Protectress of Humanity, and, further up, a larger mosaic of the Holy Transfiguration.

Each of the side towers stands 150 feet high. The south tower is dedicated to King David, from whose line Christ did come into the world. Inside the tower will be the Chapel of the Blessed Virgin Mary. The north tower is named the Tower of St. Michael the Archangel, the eternal defender of heaven against the powers of darkness, and will contain the Chapel of the Sacred Heart of Jesus.

The cathedral is designed in traditional cruciform with a 60-foot high nave crossed by a transept. The length from the front door to the wall of the sanctuary is 206 feet. The floor of the nave slopes slightly down to the area of the transept beneath the huge central dome. On the cupola of the dome will be depicted Christ the Pantocrator (The Lord of All). Six columns support the vault of the nave, and four massive columns support the central dome.

There will be a chapel on either side of the transept. On the north side will be the Chapel of Saints Peter and Paul, the two great apostles of the Church. On the south will be the Chapel of Saints Cyril and Methodius, the apostles of the Slovaks and the Slavs.

From the floor of the nave, five steps ascend to the sanctuary where the main altar will be of stone. Eventually, an iconostasis, the large and elaborately decorated icon screen of Eastern churches, will separate the congregation from the sanctuary. On the immense wall rising into the vaulted ceiling behind the altar will be an icon of the Theotokos, the Mother of God with the Christ Child. Mary occupies a central place both in the art and theology of Eastern Christianity. She is honoured as the Mediatrix between God and man and as the instrument of the salvation of the world.

His Holiness, Pope John Paul II consecrated the Cathedral of the Transfiguration in the midst of its construction during his visit to Canada in September, 1984. This marked the first time a Roman Pontiff blessed a church in North America.

Background Information:

Slovak Catholics of the Byzantine Rite

The Catholic Church encompasses different rites, which are the outward expression of a people's faith. Christianity spread throughout Europe by means of both the Roman and the Greek cultures. The faithful of the Byzantine Rite, which grew out of the Greek culture, form the second largest group in the Catholic Church after the Latin, or Roman, Rite.

The Slovak Catholics of the Byzantine Rite are the direct descendants of Cyrillomethodian-Byzantine Christianity. They received this heritage of faith and its outward expression as it was first brought to Great Moravia (which includes the territory of present-day Slovakia) in 863 A.D. by Sts. Cyril and Methodius. The Old Slavonic Liturgy and offices, which the brothers so precisely and poetically translated from the original Greek, are preserved and chanted by Slovak Byzantine Catholics as they were in the 9th century.

In 1980, Pope John Paul II named Sts. Cyril and Methodius co-patron saints of Europe. The same year, the Holy Father established an Eparchy (Diocese) for Slovaks of the Byzantine Rite in Canada, naming it after Sts. Cyril and Methodius. In 1984, Pope John Paul further demonstrated his concern and support for the Slovak people by blessing their new cathedral during his Canadian visit.

This was a great moment for Slovaks suffering religious persecution behind the Iron Curtain. Since the government has refused to invite the Pontiff to Czechoslovakia, the faithful there could, at least, be inspired and encouraged by his presence among the Slovaks in the free world.

There are 350,000 Slovak Byzantine Catholics living in Czechoslovakia, primarily in Eastern Slovakia; 30,000 live in Canada.

5. Selling a Product: Introducing "An Important Device for Athletes"

Howard Fisher, a Toronto chiropractor, wanted to promote his latest invention: the Back Strip, a firm, but flexible foam cushion designed to reduce the risk of back injury by athletes playing demanding contact sports such as hockey and football.

He couldn't afford to buy advertising in volumes that would effectively promote his invention, so he chose, instead, to generate news coverage about it.

Strategy Ideally, the thing to do when promoting a product is to get third-party endorsement. Your message will be much more credible when a recognized authority whose objectivity is beyond question touts the virtues of your invention. It would be great to get, say, a recognized sports figure to act as spokesperson by giving media interviews and appearing on public platforms. But with athletes commanding payment for public endorsements that often climbs to seven figures, that is not always feasible.

So Howard did the next best thing. He persuaded a couple of National Hockey League players to try out the Back Strip and got permission to use their brief testimonials in a news release.

The standing of the Back Strip now assured, we set about our primary goal of getting media coverage for Howard's invention, without spending an arm and a leg in the process.

Our target audiences were easy to identify: any primary- or secondary-school boy or girl who played contact sports; their parents; hockey and football coaches at primary and secondary schools and universities and in the myriad amateur leagues across the country; professional athletes and coaches; and physiotherapists, chiropractors and other health care professionals who would treat sports-related back injuries.

Our targeted media included the daily press, community newspapers, trade magazines and radio and television stations.

Procedure   We produced a comprehensive media kit that contained a news release that focused on how the Back Strip would help prevent sports injuries and included quotes from an established NHL player and trainer. Also in the kit were photographs showing the player being checked while wearing the Back Strip during an NHL game; a fact sheet on the Back Strip; biographical sketches of Howard Fisher and Michael Finewax, his business partner and marketer; and testimonials.

If the media chose to run the news release and nothing more, that was fine with us. But one of our key objectives was to arrange interviews for Howard and thus get much more extensive and varied media coverage.

To achieve this, we topped the media kit off with a personalized letter addressed individually to sports editors, medical writers and assignment or news editors at our targeted media. The kits were mailed or hand delivered and, a few days later, Michael Finewax followed up by phone to arrange interviews. The product was legitimate, the endorsements gave it credibility and the news release pinpointed a persuasive news angle.

The result was that Howard gave more than 50 interviews.

FOR IMMEDIATE RELEASE

Canadian chiropractor invents spinal pad to reduce sports injuries

TORONTO, June 20, 1988 – A prominent Canadian chiropractor has invented an innovative protective pad that will significantly reduce spinal injuries in contact sports.

The Back Strip, developed by Dr. Howard Fisher of Toronto, is expected to become standard equipment for players in high contact sports such as football, hockey and lacrosse.

"Few people realize that the spine has less natural protection than the head," Dr. Fisher says. "If you wouldn't play a contact sport without a helmet, you shouldn't be playing it without spinal protection."

The Back Strip is especially effective for children involved in contact sports, where the potential for spinal injury is high.

The Back Strip will be available in retail stores across Canada in mid-July, in time for both the football and hockey seasons.

Dr. Fisher says he designed the Back Strip to absorb the sharp initial impact of a blow and spread the focus of the force over a wider area of the back.

"It's this diffusion of the force of the blow that greatly reduces the chance of injury to the vulnerable spinal region," Dr. Fisher says.

That ability has been recognized by several National Hockey League players who wear the Back Strip to protect them from crosschecks and sudden blows when they are checked into the boards.

"It's a very good protective device, particularly for 'marked' players such as Michel Goulet and Jeff Jackson," says Jacques Lavergne, physiotherapist and trainer for the NHL's Quebec Nordiques. Russ Courtnall of the Toronto Maple Leafs also uses the Back Strip.

All three players have worn the Back Strip during games, and Goulet credits the protective device with saving him from serious injury.

"I get hit a lot when I rush up and down the ice, and the Back Strip really protects me," he says. "I remember one time this past season – (Borje) Salming put me into the crossbar, and who know what would have happened if I wasn't wearing the Back Strip."

-30-

Contact: Michael Finewax (416) 660-0020

Back Strip Fact Sheet

What

Back Strip is a new concept in protective equipment designed to reduce the effects of low-velocity trauma to the spinal area of the back, from the base of the neck to the base of the tailbone. The equipment affords no protection to the neck.

Why

Until the invention of the Back Strip, the spinal region of the back was one of the few areas of the body, excluding the neck, that was less-than-adequately protected by available equipment. The body's functions are totally controlled by the nervous system. Damage to the spine could have severe effects, including permanent paralysis. The Back Strip is intended to prevent such injuries.

How

The Back Strip absorbs the initial impact of a trauma and diffuses the force of the blow by spreading it over a much greater area.

Features

The Back Strip pad consists of a combination of layers of plastic and cross-linked closed cell foam. The Back Strip is lightweight. It conforms to the natural spinal curves of the back and is both comfortable and flexible.

Applications
The Back Strip is easy to put on. Simply step through the leg loops and fasten the waist straps and the chest and shoulder harness to secure in place.

Availability
The Back Strip is distributed by Back Strip Canada Inc., (416) 660-0020, and is available at most local sporting goods stores.

Howard Fisher, B.Sc., B.Ed., D.C.
Biography
Dr. Howard Fisher, a prominent Toronto chiropractor, is the founder and operator of the Glen Park Chiropractic Clinic. He also lectures on chiropractic and has written several articles on the subject for trade publications.

Dr. Fisher is a member of the Canadian Chiropractic Association, the Ontario Chiropractic Association, the American Chiropractic Association and the American National Strength and Conditioning Association. He received his B.Sc. and B.Ed. degrees from the University of Toronto and his D.C. cum laude from the Canadian Memorial Chiropractic College.

In addition to his career in chiropractic, Dr. Fisher is an avid athlete and coaches several youth teams. He has also co-authored several movies and a television series.

A dynamic and colourful personality, Dr. Fisher resides in Thornhill, Ontario, with his wife and their two children.

Michael Finewax, B.A.
Biography
Michael Finewax is an established sports journalist who has written extensively for publications in Canada and abroad. He is also the author of several screenplays and is currently working on a novel.

In addition to his writing, Mr. Finewax serves as a volunteer for the Variety Club and coaches men's baseball and children's softball teams. He currently resides in Mississauga, Ont.

Mr. Finewax is a graduate of York University with a Bachelor's degree in history and continues to enrol in journalism courses.

What the players say about the Back Strip

"The people I hit will need this."
  Leo Ezerins, outside linebacker, Hamilton Tiger Cats

"I don't have to be extra cautious, because it cuts down on the pain or shock from the crosschecks and hitting your back along the boards."
  Jeff Jackson, forward, Quebec Nordiques

"It is made for everybody, not just for the superstar, but for the weekend athletes, too. [It] will be the perfect spinal protector."
  Jacques Lavergne, physiotherapist, trainer, Quebec Nordiques

"I get hit a lot when I rush up and down the ice, and the Back Strip really protects me."
  Michel Goulet, Quebec Nordiques

What the doctors say about the Back Strip

"The real danger in contact or collision sports is damage to the epiphyseal growth plate (the centre growth in the bone) and certainly the Back Strip is an important protective device against this type of injury in adolescents."
  Dr. Steward A. O'Brien, B.A., B.PHE., B.Ed., D.C., F.C.C.S.S. and a former offensive lineman in the Canadian Football League

"I see this spinal pad being made mandatory for anyone playing contact sport in the future. It is a product that has been needed for some time. . . and finally has arrived."
  Dr. Howard B. Wernick M.D., Phoenix, Arizona

"This spinal pad will effectively reduce the effects of low-velocity trauma to the spine, common in contact sports."
  Dr. Michael West M.D., orthopedic surgeon in Toronto

The common thread running through each of these programs is the newsworthiness of the subject matter. The projects succeeded, not because the media relations practitioner created news out of nothing, but because the media relations practitioner identified what was inherently newsworthy about the situations. It's in much the same way that geologists don't create gold, silver or copper, but rather discover existing metals and minerals that are hidden by a shroud of overburden and waste rock.

To carry the mining analogy a step further, to identify what is newsworthy and then stop there would be like the geologist discovering an orebody and then walking away. To complete the job successfully, the ore must be mined, processed and brought to market. Likewise, as a media relations practitioner, you must develop the news into a useful product that satisfies both the requirements of the working media and the goals and objectives of your organization. And then you must get that product into the hands of the media – your market.

That is what managing the media is all about.

Photo Credits